EVOLUTION OF ANCIENT INDIAN LAW

EVOLUTION OF ANCIENT INDIAN LAW

NARES CHANDRA SENGUPTA

GYAN

Published by

Gyan Publishing House
5, Ansari Road
Daryaganj, New Delhi-110002
Phone: 011-47034999, 9811692060
E-mail: books@gyanbooks.com

Distribution Network
gyanbooks.com
India, USA, Canada, UK, Australia

ISBN: 978-93-6920-077-1 (HB)

First Published, 1950

2nd Impression 2026

Printed at: Gyan Press, Delhi.

EVOLUTION OF ANCIENT INDIAN LAW
Author: NARES CHANDRA SENGUPTA

EVOLUTION OF ANCIENT INDIAN LAW

NARES CHANDRA SEN-GUPTA, M.A., LL.D.,

Senior Advocate, Supreme Court of India, Advocate, Calcutta High Court, Tagore Law Professor 1950, Late Dean of the Faculty of Law, University of Dacca, Author of "Sources of Law and Society in Ancient India", "Evolution of Law", "Pratnavidhana", etc., etc.

PREFACE TO THE THIRD EDITION

This book was published more than thirty-seven years ago, and received flattering commendation from competent scholars and reviewers in India and abroad. It has been out of print for a number of years, but I deferred publishing a new edition in the hope of making very considerable improvement and enlargement.

Circumstances have prevented the compilation of the more ambitious work I had in view and I am not sure when I shall be able to prepare the larger work. I have, therefore, decided to publish the original work with only slight alterations, some of them suggested by criticisms on the work.

I hope that this work may be of some help to students and scholars engaged in the study of this fascinating though somewhat baffling subject.

Calcutta
2. 6. 62

N. C. S-G.

CONTENTS

THE EVOLUTION OF LAW

CHAPTER I

SCOPE, PROVINCE AND MATERIALS FOR THE STUDY OF SOCIOLOGICA JURISPRUDENCE

THE NAME OF THE SUBJECT : The subject-matter of this work is what may be called a study of laws in their evolution, not the laws of any particular country or particular age but human laws generally. It may be called Historical Jurisprudence or Comparative Jurisprudence ; but both these terms are liable to misconstruction, because they have been applied to other branches of the study of Law. A more satisfactory term is Sociological Jurisprudence, though that too is not perfect.

PURPOSE OF THE STUDY : In this study we take our stand on the fact that human society grows, no matter whether you take the most forward races of the civilised world, or the most backward savages. Society, even among savages, does not stand now where it did in the days of the first man. The society and institutions that you find there are the results of a long course of evolution. It is the purpose of Sociology to study this evolution of the various social forms and institutions.

SOURCES OF INFORMATION : There are two main sources of information with regard to the earlier stages in the study of this evolution : (*i*) the ancient social history of civilised communities and (*ii*) condition of the societies of retarded races, who have in many cases retained the primitive institutions which have died out in civilised society.

OF ANCIENT SOCIETY, (1) WRITTEN ACCOUNTS LEFT BY THE PEOPLE THEMSELVES : So far as the past history of civilised races is concerned, information about it may be obtained from three different sources. Firstly, there are accounts left of the society of ancient times by the people themselves. Such accounts may be found from very remote time. The *Iliad* and the *Odyssey*, the *Mahabharata* and the *Ramayana*, the Norwegian and Icelandic Sagas and all the other legendary lore of different communities furnish such material. Of a somewhat different kind, though belonging to the same category are ancient historical records like those of Herodotus and Thucydides. The value of such records where they exist, is necessarily very great. But we have to set off against this the aberrations caused by various circumstances. Racial pride very often deflects the judgment of the authors. Besides, these ancient works often give us society as it ought to be according to the authors, rather than society as it actually is. Then again, there is the further fact that the very familiarity of the authors with the institutions they are dealing with, makes them blind to many things in them which they take for granted.

(2) ACCOUNTS OF FOREIGN OBSERVERS: In the second place there are records of the institutions left by foreign observers. These have the merit of absence of bias in favour of the society described. But on the other hand there is the opposite bias arising from a sense of racial pride, which looks upon institutions differing from those of the observer's own society with more or less contempt. Even Cæsar and Tacitus, the most faithful recorders of foreign customs we know of, are not quite free from this bias, though Tacitus sometimes goes to the other extreme of praising German customs to discredit the Roman society of his time. The foreign observer has the advantage of observing many things which escape the observation of the local recorders by reason of their very familiarity. On the other hand foreigners can seldom enter into the spirit of foreign institutions to the same extent as local observers may. The result very often is that, with the best of intentions, they give very distorted descriptions of institutions. These are the natural pitfalls of a thoroughly honest foreign observer. Besides, foreign observers often write with a purpose, whether, as in that entirely imaginative work, Xenophon's *Cyropaedia*, with the object of idealising foreign institutions by way of criticism of those of the writer's own country or for the purpose of glorifying the national institutions of the observer, as in the description of Troglodytes or Cyclops by Herodotus and Homer.

(3) ANCIENT LAW: From all these defects of the local records, the last source of information about ancient societies,

namely, laws, are exempt. They are, as Maine points out, the unconscious records, faithfully kept, of the ancient institutions of the race. They were made, not for the purpose of being passed on to posterity as a picture of the society of the time, but with the practical object of regulating contemporary society. They are therefore absolutely free from bias ; so that, if we can get hold of a body of laws of any race at a particular age, we may be perfectly sure that the institutions vouched for by those laws actually existed in the society of that age. A study of ancient laws therefore is of much greater importance in the study of the social history of a race and of the evolution of society.

NEED OF CAUTION IN DEALING WITH ANCIENT LAW : SURVIVALS IN LAW BOOKS : We have to be cautious however and make sure that the laws we are dealing with are really laws of that particular age. The mere fact that a rule is found in the law books of a particular time does not necessarily imply that the law was actually in existence at that time. Laws and institutions of ancient times have often a habit of lingering in the books long after they have ceased to have any practical value. If you take up a text-book on Hindu Law written, say, one hundred years ago, you will find it dealing with the institution of *Niyoga*, with marriages outside caste, with the eight forms of marriage and twelve forms of sons, sometimes without giving you the slightest suggestion that they were obsolete. Long after the son's and the wife's right to separate property had been recognised in Hindu Law and embodied, in fact, in other parts of the same work, we find Manu laying down that sons, slaves and wives were incapable of acquiring property, and that whatever they acquired became the property of him to whom they belonged. This text survived because it was still living authority in respect of the slave though it had become quite obsolete in the case of the others. Nor is this defect one of very ancient laws alone. As late as in the days of Queen Victoria, it was discovered that trial by battle which had, for centuries, ceased to be practical law but never formally repealed was still good law according to the books.

IDEAL CHARACTER OF SOME LAWS : On the other hand there are laws which lay down what ought to be, rather than what are practical laws. The Hindu Codes, specially the later ones, are full of laws of this character. If we were to draw a sketch of society on the basis of these idealistic laws, it would naturally represent something very different from the actual state of affairs. While therefore the very great importance of laws for studying the societies in ancient times cannot be gainsaid, the path of such study is not exactly a bed of roses. A great deal of circumspection has to be exercised for determining what exactly are the laws of any particular race or age before we can proceed to dogmatise about them.

MAINE, THE FATHER OF COMPARATIVE JURISPRUDENCE : The credit for drawing attention, of the English-speaking world at least, to the importance of a study of laws on the genetic method belongs to Sir Henry Maine. He established the new school of historico-comparative jurisprudence by his researches which are embodied in four volumes of epoch-making works. The materials then at his disposal were exceedingly scanty. Such facts as were known had never before been critically investigated. The result is that you will find many of Maine's conclusions requiring revision now. But the new line of study which he initiated was full of the richest promise. Since his days, a great deal has been done by other scholars following in his wake. But considering the very limited evidence which was accessible to him, the wonder is not that Maine's conclusions will require correction at times, but that so much of his conclusions is actually supported and strengthened by later researches.

IHERING AND HIS METHOD : At the same time with Maine, there was another great jurist in Germany who also studied ancient laws on very similar lines. That was Rudolph von Ihering. There is a fundamental difference however between the methods of Ihering and Maine. Both studied historical facts and tried to arrive at the course of their evolution. But while Maine's method was mainly empirical, Ihering's was one in the nature of a critical study of those facts. In his book on the Spirit of Roman Law (*Geist der Römischen Rechts*) he points out that the object of the historical jurist is not to study the external history of legal institutions but their inner chronology, that is to say, their inner evolution. He points out also how, as a matter of fact, chronological sequence of facts and institutions very often gives an erroneous impression of their genetic order. The true method for him therefore was to interrogate the historical facts critically for the purpose of arriving at the inner evolution of juridical phenomena by searching, in the inner motives of their being, for their hidden springs and ultimate roots and their spiritual interdependence.[1]

Since Maine and Ihering wrote, the study has flourished very much. Fustel de Coulanges, Letourneau, Kohler, Tarde and a large body of other scholars have devoted themselves to the study of juristic evolution with considerable ability and often with command of a vast deal more of material than was available either to Maine or to Ihering.

ROMAN LAW AND ITS IMPORTANCE: First amongst the ancient laws we may name Roman law, not because it is anything near the earliest system, but because it has the longest ascertainable history of any legal system. And, besides, Roman law has been studied for centuries and the acutest minds have been devoted to the study of the history of Roman laws and institutions. The result is that we can speak with far greater assurance of the development of laws and institutions in Rome than of those of any other country. Besides, the methodical treatment of laws in Rome and the systematic history that we have got of the greater part of the legal life of Rome marks it out easily as the standard by reference to which we may study other legal systems.

LAWS OF THE HELLENES: The laws of the Hellenes form also an important part of the body of ancient laws to which we have access. The sources of information with reference to this law are far fewer than in the case of Rome. We have got the Code of Solon and the speeches of orators made in defence of accused persons before the Athenian tribunal, for instance.

---

1 Ihering, *Geist der Romischen*, Vol. 1, p. 15. * * * Was sie beabsichtigt ist eine Kritik der Romischen Rechts * * * * eine geschichtsphilosophische Kritik, d. h. eine solche. welche dasselbe auf seinem ganzen Wege von Anfang bis zu Ende begleitet, nicht um sich bei der aussern historischen Tatsache zu begnugen * * * sondern um das innere Getriebe des geschichtlichen Werdens, die verborgenen Triebfedern, die letzten Grunde, den geistigen Zusammenhang der gesamten Rechtsentwicklung zu ergrunden.

EGYPTIAN AND BABYLONIAN LAW : The Egyptian Law leads us back to a very remote antiquity of which we have got a fairly accurate record. But so far as legal history is concerned, perhaps the most startling and the most interesting body of evidence is furnished from ancient Babylon. The laws of Babylon and their ancient documents embodying legal transaction between parties have come down to us in a form in which they could not have been tampered with. These documents consist of tablets of baked earth, upon which were inscribed the writings of the ancient Chaldeans and these tablets have been unearthed recently from where they had lain for thousands of years, unknown and away from human eyes. The excavations which were carried on in Mesopotamia in the last century led to the discovery of not only great cities and palaces but also of libraries containing numerous volumes of these earthen books and of a large number of documents which have added very greatly to our knowledge of ancient laws.

LAWS OF ISRAEL : Another ancient system of laws of which we have a great deal of information, although it is not qnite as unimpeachable as the Babylonian evidence, is that of the Hebrews. The *Old Testament* and *Talmud* between them contain a vast amount of material for legal history of this important Semitic race which has only been partially utilised.

HINDU LAW : A vast mine of information about juridical history is to be found in the ancient laws of India. The wroks which embody these laws and customs date back to very remote antiquity and embody customs and usages which have come down from a still remoter antiquity. This vast material however suffers from a great deal of confusion of sequences, so that it is very difficult to say of any law or institution that it either preceded or followed another law or institution. The whole subject has got to be studied from the really critical-historical point of view by historians of the law. And the evidences have to be critically sifted by comparison with those of other Indo-Germanic races.

LAWS OF CELTIC AND GERMANIC RACES : Amongst these a very important source of our knowledge is to be found in the laws and customs of the Celtic and Germanic races of North

Europe. We have very good accounts of the early Celtic and Germanic customs from the pen of acute observers like Julius Cæsar and Tacitus who, in those remote days obtained some first-hand knowledge of these races, who were then in a much less advanced state of civilisaiton than the Romans or Greeks. These customs also form the basis of the later laws of the Germanic races which can be studied, for instance, in the *Leges Barbarorum*, in the Anglo-Saxon laws and in the Icelandic Sagas.

LAWS OF SLAVONIC RACES : Some of the ancient customs of Indo-Germanic races have been traced in the latter-day customs of Slavonic races in Russia and the Balkan peninsula.

BREHON LAWS : A notable instance of these primitive Indo-Germanic laws is furnished by the Brehon laws. These were originally the laws of Celtic races in their pre-Christian days which were carried down from generation to generation by their priests. But in their present form they have been transformed by the influence of Christianity. Inspite of this we can trace in these laws a great deal of genuine ancient Celtic laws.

ANTHROPOLOGICAL RESEARCHES : A mass of material which has proved of incalculable use for the study of ancient laws and institutions has been supplied by modern anthropological and sociological researches. The Science of Sociology owed its origin to Comte, but it took definite shape only in the hands of Herbert Spencer who studied social institutions from the evolutionary standpoint. To him social institutions, like the vegetable and animal life, were subject to the fundamental laws of evolution. This thesis Spencer established in his great work, the *Principles of Sociology*. And he laid the foundation of a much more exact and scientific study of primitive institutions by the undertaking, which was started under his supervision in the first instance, of a Descriptive Sociology or an account of the institutions amongst the backward races of the world by first-hand investigation. This work has since been followed in a very comprehensive manner, and we have, at the present moment, a large mass of material with reference to the customs and usages of a great many backward races of Africa, America, India, Arabia, Australasia and elsewhere.

These studies of the institutions of retarded races have the greatest value for the study of the evolution of Law ; because these often represent the earlier stages in the social history of the advanced races. We must not make the mistake however of assuming that these races as they stand at the present day represent the absolutely primitive man. They also have had a history of thousands of years, in the course of which their customs and usages have also been modified, by the influence of neighbours, by admixture of races as well as by mere natural developments, though the changes have been far less pronounced than the changes amongst the advanced races. So the mere fact that we find institutions amongst a race who are in a very backward state of civilisation does not necessarily imply that the institution was an absolutely primitive one. We have to recollect that these institutions as we now have them amongst the savage races represent the result of evolution for thousands of years in their own way. Studied with this precaution in mind, these institutions are likely to throw a considerable amount of light upon the primitive history of legal institutions among advanced races.

CHAPTER II

Section I—METHOD OF STUDY

CHRONOLOGY OF ANCIENT LAW BOOKS. ITS IMPORTANCE AND WEIGHT : In dealing with ancient laws and the customs and usages of retarded races it is of the utmost importance to have a clear idea of the method to be followed in studying them. So far as systems of law are concerned, they have to be studied in the order of their evolution. For such a study it is very important to have a clear idea of the chronology of the documents in which those laws are found. At the same time it must not be understood that the chronology of such works, even when well understood, is necessarily identical with the history of the evolution of the laws. Ihering in his *Spirit of Roman Law* gives a very necessary warning against being misled by the mere sequence of the legal works into assuming that they necessarily embody legal institutions in the order of their evolution. Early *Rechtssätze* (expressions of law), he says, are like the first attempts of people to draw ; their imperfection arises from two circumstances : (1) defects in powers of observation, (2) defects in powers of expression. Ancient laws often omit to state rules of law, not because those rules were not in fact in force in those times, but because either from over-familiarity with them contemporary legislators failed to notice their existence, or they took them for granted and did not think it necessary to mention them. Apart from this, the ancients did not always succeed in giving full expression to the law that they actually found in existence and wanted to express. Sometimes their expression of the law was too wide and, by omitting to state the necessary qualifications of the rule, included things which they did not contemplate, and at other times the exposition was too narrow and did not include many things which they actually wanted to include. The difference necessitated the growth of a law of interpretation. The early interpreters of law, once it had been imposed in a satisfactory form of words, would not have the liberty of changing the words as a modern legislature has. At the same time where they found the words actually embodying a law which was at variance with the acutal law, they purported to *interpret* the law so that it should have the exact meaning that it was desired to have. The early expressions of law also suffer from another serious defect, namely, that the law-givers very often lay down, not what is the actual law, but what they want to be the law. In other words, they are prompted by a desire to improve the society on the lines of their ideals though the ideal might not have been immediately realised in society and sometimes was never realised at all.

PRECAUTIONS TO BE TAKEN IN THE STUDY OF ANCIENT LAWS : The result of all these circumstances is that the early statements of law give an imperfect idea of the actual law of the time. The historical student of law has therefore to examine these early codes of law very critically, so that they may arrive at a correct appreciation of the right laws of any time.

SIMILARITIES IN LAWS AND GUSTOMS OF DIFFERENT RACES : In studying ancient systems of law, as well as the institutions and custom of retarded races one meets very often with similarities not only in institutions and customs but also, sometimes, in the course of their evolution. These similarities form in fact the particular material on which the sciences of Anthropology and Sociological Jurisprudence are based.

THEY DO NOT NECESSARILY IMPLY BORROWING : These similarities very often arise from imitation or borrowing. The results of anthropological researches have shown most astounding instances of borrowing as between races apparently vary far from one another. But it must not be supposed that, in every case, a similarity of laws and institutions or history necessarily indicates borrowing. There was too great a tendency in the last century to regard all cases of similarities as cases of borrowing or conscious imitation. Anthropology, since then, has proved that very similar institutions and practices can arise and have actually arisen, quite independently in entirely distinct societies of men. The foundation of this fact lies in the essential similarity of human nature. All men are more or less prompted by certain common natural desires, emotions and volitional tendencies. Society like every other human institution, originates in the effort of the human mind to satisfy these natural cravings. It very often happens that there are very few possible modes of satisfying these wants and, if two human societies, limited in the choice of the methods of satisfying their wants, sometimes stumble upon the same identical device for satisfying that want, it is not a fact to be wondered at. Therefore, similarities may arise not only from imitation or borrowing, but also by way of spontaneous evolution from very natural impulses. This fact will have to be constantly borne in mind by the student of Comparative Historical Jurisprudence. It may be laid down as a safe rule for such a student that where an institution or a law can be explained as having its origin in spontaneous evolution it would be rash to imagine that there has been a borrowing of anything from other societies. It is only when the evidence of such borrowing is clear or such phenomena cannot be explained on the hypothesis of spontaneous evolution, that a theory of borrowing can be justified.

ANCIENT LAW AND ANCIENT SOCIETY : In studying ancient and primitive law we must remember that law is at no time self-sufficient. It is only one part of the total body of rules of conduct affecting men in the society in which it prevails. To get a correct appreciation of the real position and effect of any provision of ancient law, therefore, we have very often to take it along with the entire life of the people. Thus, one would get an altogether erroneous view of the position of the father in ancient Rome, or for that matter in ancient India, if one proceeded solely on the basis of the provisions in the law proper without taking into consideration, in Rome for instance, of the *Fas* and *Boni mores*. So also in other cases, underneath everything that is said in law, there are a great many silent presuppositions which were understood by contemporaries but which are not necessarily laid down in the laws. The historical student of law, in order to be quite accurate, has to get as correct an appreciation as possible of these underlying presuppositions of the laws of the society he is studying. Conclusions based upon the laws alone without taking adequate account of these underlying presuppositions of the laws are likely to lead to wholly erroneous conclusions. It is, no doubt, very difficult to get a perfectly accurate idea of these ancient social concepts and institutions which will supply the necessary corrective to the law. But by a study of these ancient laws on the comparative method and by bringing to the aid of this study all that is known of ancient social history and of the social evolution of primitive or retarded races, it is often possible at the present day to arrive at a fair idea of the background of social institutions against which we have to place the laws in order to get them in their true perspective. Very often the true motive underlying an institution which remains unexplained in one society will be found to be supplied by the laws of another society or by customs, institutions and ideas of a retarded race of the present day. But we must remember that so long as we cannot have a really correct idea of the ancient society whose laws we are studying, our conclusions with regard to the evolution of that law must be considered tentative.

THE EVOLUTION OF LAW NOT UNIFORM EVERYWHERE: Another precaution which it is absolutely necessary to bear in mind is that we must not attempt to construct too hastily a common course of evolution of the laws of the whole world. Human society has not progressed all over on the same lines. There have been widely varying institutions to start with, and institutions have often progressed along widely different lines in different communities. It is not possible therefore to do now what Maine attempted to do, at any rate, in his earliest work, and others have attempted to do in other connections,[1] namely, to construct a single course of evolution for all human institutions of primitive times. There have been different lines of progress. Generalising from those various lines of evolution must land us in more or less abstract theories for which it will be difficult to find counterparts in facts.

GREAT GROUPS OF THE HUMAN RACE: Though generalisation on such a wide scale must be considered very risky, within narrower limits such generalisation may be attempted with greater confidence. For it is possible, to classify the human race into certain large groups within which social evolution

1 For instance McLennan in *Primitive Marriage*, Fustel de Coulanges in *The Ancient City*, and also to some extent Kohler in *Philosophy of Law*.

has been more or less similar, and the evolution has been prompted by more or less similar underlying ideas and principles.

Since Bopp discovered a fundamental unity between Indo-Germanic races by a comparative study of their languages which was attributed to an original Aryan race spreading over the greater part of Europe and Asia, a more intensive study of the races by Anthropology has shown that the raçial unity of origin of these races is not so well founded. But while the exaggerated conclusions of a racial origin of these cultures have to be discarded in favour of a great admixture of races and cultures among them, the existence of a common, though possibly mixed, cultural basis of these several races in pre-historic times stands established. Similarly there is a fundamental cultural unity amongst the great Semitic races, as also amongst the Mongolian races. No doubt our conclusions even with regard to these families of human race have to be corrected by reference to Anthropology. Yet in studying the social and legal histories of these races, we are on much surer ground when we generalise, than when we dogmatise about one general course of evolution of the laws and institutions of the whole human race.

Section II—Forms of Laws

Maine's theory of the evolution of forms of law: At the present day we find laws mostly embodied in written documents whether they are codes, books of case-law or scientific treatises on law. To some extent also laws are found in customs and usages. But in ancient times, the forms of law were not identical with those of the laws of the present day. Maine in his *Ancient Law* develops a theory of the evolution of the forms of law. According to him, general propositions of law are later than specific decisions on particular points.

Themistes: The oldest form of law in the world according to him is represented in the Themistes referred to by Homer. These are really decisions or judgements given on particular cases brought before the Chief for decision, the judgement being supposed in every instance to have been derived by direct inspiration from the Gods.

Dike : These Themistes however by repetition developed into more or less general rules of rudimentary custom which are also expressed by the Homeric term Dike. So long as society was organised on a monarchical basis, the form of law was always of this type and every law was supposed to be the result of a direct inspiration of the King. Monarchs however were everywhere superseded in course of time, by aristocracies of some sort. The remarkable pre-eminence of the Chief which alone maintained the authority of the absolute chieftain did not generally continue in his successors, and, naturally, the authority of weak and incapable chiefs tended to grow less and less. They were therefore supplanted by aristocracy everywhere in ancient society.

Transition to aristocracy, Customary Law : There were various forms of aristocracy. In some, as in Sparta or India the form of monarchy was retained but the real power passed from the hands of the King to a body of men who by reason of their descent and their power claimed to dominate the state. In others again as in Athens or Rome even the semblance of monarchy was dispensed with and the authority vested formally as well as really in the aristocrats themselves. In some places the aristocracy consisted of military classes, in others it was chiefly of the spiritual or intellectual classes. But everywhere the authority passed from the King to a privileged class. This change corresponded, according to Maine, to a change in the nature of law. The aristocrats or the class in whom the authority in respect of laws now vested could not claim the same direct inspiration which it was possible for the sacred person, the King, to claim. The progress of society likewise had made it impossible to sustain the theory of direct inspiration, as, by this time, laws had come to be understood as more or less general rules. These aristocrats therefore claimed, not a direct inspiration from the Gods, but a monopoly of the traditional knowledge of the laws which was handed down in their families from generation to generation. This therefore is the second stage in the evolution of the forms of law namely the age of customary law.

Codes : In course of time however this stage is replaced by the third stage, that of the Codes. Most civilised ancient societies, at some stage or other of their evolution, had their codes. The causes which led to the writing out of the customary law, which was all that these ancient codes purported to be, were various. In most cases the laws were recorded for the purpose of assisting the memory of the aristocratic law-givers and were maintained as manuals in use in their schools. But in Rome, and possibly in some other places, the code was the result of the rise of democracy. The people wanted to know the law and insisted upon those laws being inscribed in a more or less public form. The Code did so in Rome, but not in ancient India, where the first codes were really manuals for use of the learned men who laid down the law and for the instruction of their pupils. Maine however notices one common factor among the reasons which led to the evolution of codes in different places, namely, the spread of the art of writing. The codes according to him always came into existence when the art of writing became familiar to the people.

FURTHER DEVELOPMENT OF LAW—FICTION, EQUITY, LEGISLATION : When once the codes were formulated, the further spontaneous development of law ceased. It no longer developed of itself, it was deliberately changed and developed. The processes by which the further development of law takes place according to Maine are Fiction, Equity and Legislation. These three processes were utilised one after another in course of the gradual evolution of laws.

Fiction : By fiction Maine understands the change made in the law laid down in the written code under cover of the assumption that it is not being changed but only applied in specific cases. The most notable instance of fiction in the history of law is the fiction of interpretation. In Rome as well as in India this fiction was carried to a very high degree of subtlety by a body of jurists, who were not vested with any legislative or judicial authority, but whose opinions gained currency by reason of the eminence and learning of the persons laying down the law. In England the same thing has been done from the reign of Edward I, but not by the same agency. Law has been authoritatively laid down by English courts in judicial decisions in which they purported merely to interpret the old law, but, in point of fact, often laid down new law which was considered to be binding on all courts of equal or inferior jurisdiction. Students of law are all familiar with the idea of the development of law by means of the fiction of interpretation in English case-law, the Roman *Responsa Prudentum* and the commentaries and *Nibandhas* of Hindu Law.

Equity : Fiction is replaced gradually in Roman Law by another principle, namely, Equity. In England also the same agency was availed of by the Chancellors for the purpose of ameliorating the Law. In Rome the Prætor purported to ameliorate the law in the course of its administration by an appeal to the Law of Nature or Equity which was supposed to be a principle of universal application with inherent power to override the written Law. This principle of a natural justice having claims to remove the imperfection of the common or civil law does not appear to have been very much utilised elsewhere. But Maine believes that it was a necessary step in the progress from fiction to legislation. The characteristic of Equity as an instrument for the improvement of law lies in this that its interference with the previous law is express and avowed, whereas in fiction it is not so. The basis of the authority of the new law is supposed to be a principle of higher worth, superior to the authority of the existing laws, while in legislation the authority of the new law arises not from the inherent nature of the principle but from the authority of the agency laying down the law.

Legislation : Legislation stands for the comparatively late method of laying down the law by the authority of the sovereign. While ancient codes were merely declaratory of the customary law, the legislation of later days involved the introduction of new law which added to or superseded the old law by a deliberate act of the Sovereign. This weapon is not found to be used for the changing of the law until the society gets used to the idea that law is changeable, by the application of the other principles.

CRITICISM OF MAINE'S THEORY. RELIGIOUS LAW EXISTED BEFORE CIVIL LAW : This course of evolution laid down by Maine cannot be accepted as entirely correct even in the case of Greece and Rome and does not certainly represent the course of history everywhere. Maine's fundamental error in formulating this theory seems to lie in his failure to recognise that early law is an integral part of religion.[1] In the very early days of society, law is nowhere found dissociated from religion or its predecessor, magic, which, with its own ideas of right and wrong already held the ground before law as such came into existence. The religious law had an organisation for enforcing, supporting and explaining it. When, at a later date, the jurist's law first came into existence, it was this organisation which took charge of it. Thus in the Greece of Homer, the king was the chief of religion as well as of the military organisation. It was nothing unusual therefore that when a question of right and wrong arose, these people brought it before the king for adjudication. Under similar circumstances in the India of the Vedic age, people would go, not to the king but more readily to the *Parishad*[2] which laid down the religious Law for the people. While therefore the roots of adjudication and Law in Greece might lead us back to the *Themis* of the King, in India it would lead us back to a body of men who had made the pursuit of learning their vocation in life, and who constituted the Assembly or *Parishad* who were already judges of the religious life of the people.

ADJUDICATION PRESUPPOSES A BASIS OF RULES OF JUSTICE : To me it seems altogether erroneous to assume that adjudication could have preceded Law unless you take Law in a very narrow sense. That a dispute is brought before any body for adjudication or the determination of the justice of the thing implies that people have already got an idea of justice in

1 Fustel de Coulanges in his *Ancient City* emphasises the importance of religion and religious laws in primitive and ancient society. There is room for suspicion that the importance of religion in the constitution and evolution of Greek, Roman and Indian societies has been exaggerated by him. But the general thesis that religion underlies most ancient laws and institutions cannot be gainsaid. Maine himself refers to the religious character of ancient law in his *Early Law and Custom*. See also Leist, *Altarisches Jus Gentium*, p. 77 ff.

2 On the constitution and history of the *Parishad*, see Sen Gupta, *Sources of Law and Society in Ancient India* (*Calcutta University*).

human relations and it is that justice or *Dharma* which they want to enforce by means of the adjudication. Even before the first adjudication, therefore, there must have existed a conception of a rule of justice which was at that time supplied by *Fas* or *Dharma* or *Rita*. In course of time, as adjudication develops, these rules of justice tend to become more and more crystallised, diversified and defined till they lead, in some places, to the separation of law from a general code of right founded on religion.[1]

SUGGESTED ORIGIN OF ADJUDICATION : Adjudication is so far from being the primary fact in jurisprudence that it has itself got a history behind it. Long before there was any possibility for adjudication, people used to right their wrongs by self-help. Their ideas of justice were rudimentary and they were more guided by the desire for revenge than by anything else. In seeking to right one's wrong by self-help a man in primitive society could get the support of his family and clan. But so soon as self-help becomes something other than remedy by one's own effort, so soon, in fact, as you have to get other people, whether in your family or in your *gens* or clan, to identify themselves with you in seeking redress, you have to step beyond the bare principle of revenge. It would not now be enough that you feel a desire to do somebody an injury, but there must be circumstances in the case which, in the opinion of your family or your clan, justifies your seeking to injure your enemy. It is from this that a rudimentary idea of justice may be said to grow. That reprisal is just which would induce your family or clansmen to join in seeking vengeance with you. This rudimentary conception of justice becomes crystallised in many communities in the law of justified revenge which is known as the *Lex talionis* or the law of retaliation. In the *Twelve Tables* we find it laid down that if a limb is broken or blood flows there may be retaliation. This corresponds to the Law of the *Old*

---

1 Leist, *Altarisches Jus Gentium*, p. 111, *et. seq*., speaks of a *Rita* (ratio) stage of customary law preceding the *Dharma* (Themis, fas) stage of law. Although I cannot accept the theory in the clear-cut shape in which it is presented, there is a great truth underlying this proposition.

Testament which provides "an eye for an eye and a tooth for a tooth." This law, cruel as it seems to us, represents a notable advance on the primitive instinct of vengeance, because the revenge is not now merely a private instinct ; it is regulated by some rule and some measure, however rudimentary. The stages by which this justified reprisal gradually developed through the intermediate stages of voluntary arbitration to adjudication by public judges like the king or the Prætor are matters which will have to be dealt with later on.[1] But it is perfectly clear that long before any adjudication could arise and any juridical law could be said to exist, there already existed a standard of right and wrong which was supported by the opinion of the community and which might be enforced with the aid of the community. The tribunal which adjudicates on disputes takes different shapes in different communities ; but it always adjudicates on the basis of a more or less vague notion of justified reprisal. The constitution of the tribunal differs in different parts of the world. The motives underlying the interference of the head or heads of the social organisation in private disputes were also apparently different in different communities. And it is not possible to lay down one definite course for the whole human race in respect of the origin and early history of adjudication and law.

THE LAW ADMINISTERED BASED ON SUPERNATURAL SANCTION : The law which was administered by these primitive tribunals was also different in different communities. But whatever it might have been it always proceeded on the basis of a certain body of rules of right believed to have a religious and supernatural sanction. It is hard to conceive that society at any time could have been without customary rules or that it should have arrived at a formulation of the rules only by generalisation from individual dooms. A theory like this labours under the serious defect that it fails to recognise the fact that before the lawyer's law there always existed the law of the priest. The roots of law have to be sought in the *Fas* and the *Dharma* and further back in the *Rita* or *ratio*, at any rate amongst the Aryan culture groups.

---

1 See *post*, Chapter VIII.

Customary law precedes adjudication by King in primitive Aryan Society : Maine's theories about transition from *Dike* to custom must also be corrected by the same qualification that it is not a universal law of evolution. Whatever may be said about the course of evolution in Greece or Rome it is perfectly clear that in India and, possibly, amongst the original Indo-Germanic race there never was that absolute autocratic stage which would make the stage of *Themis* or *Dike* possible. From the earliest traces that we can get of the social organisation of an Aryan race we gather that they were not governed by a king, but by a group of men, like the star-gazers described by Berosius with reference to the Kassites, who devoted themselves to the knowledge of superhuman things. We find their descendants in the later political organisation in the Magi of Persia, the Brahmins of India, the Druids and other priests of the Celtic and Teutonic races and other similar institutions. From the very earliest times the authority in society seems to have been vested in Aryan societies in such a body of men who administered the Law which they were supposed to derive from beatific vision or from tradition. This tradition represented the custom of the school of learned men and became embodied, later, in the early codes of India. So that the aristocracy seems to have been administering the law of custom and tradition from the earliest times that we can imagine amongst these people.

Note on the Origin of Custom

The origin of custom in primitive society has formed the subject of keen controversy. Tarde is of opinion that the greater part of the laws and institutions of people originated in imitation following upon invention. "Speaking, praying, working, fighting, doing whatever sort of work," says he, "involves repeating what one has learnt from one who has acquired from some one else. And so one after another back to the first framers of each word-root * * * back to the few authors of each form of rites, of each method of labour, of each mode of war, fencing boots, strategic ruses which pass from man to man, more or less prolonged." "I do not say," he continues, "that imitation is all of social reality, it is but one expression of sympathy which antedates it and which it intensifies in expressing, and it depends upon invention, the spark from which it is only the greater light."[1] This may be illustrated by reference to the growth of language. We speak the language which we have learnt partly from our parents and partly from others, which has, in fact been passed on to us from our predecessors. So also marriage customs and other rituals, and, in fact, every social institution may be shown to be evolved by imitation of others. At the same time, as Tarde intimates, imitation is not all of social reality. There is continuous invention on the part of man. An invention is imitated and often forms the root of a convention. Further, besides imitation there exists another principle, which Tarde calls Logic or the application of reason. Illustration of logical development may be found not only in the case of developed societies and institutions but also in primitive and ancient communities. When you notice a sportsman handling his bat in a particular way, you try to imitate him. But you not only imitate, you also apply your reason to decide why that particular stroke is more effective than any other. Suppose you arrive at the conclusion rightly or wrongly, that it is the swing of the bat which gives a greater force to the ball and makes the stroke more effective. You at once arrive at a principle, which you apply in other cases, as when you are handling a Tennis racket. When the primitive man applies his reason to institutions which he imitates, he does not exactly reason as we do, in terms, of the developed conceptions and highly cultivated reason of to-day but on the basis of conceptions and conventions of his day and in accordance with the modes of arguments with which he is familiar. But reasoning of some sort is operative as a social force throughout.

While thus there is a great deal of justice in Tarde's theory, there is room for saying that Tarde perhaps exaggerates, to some extent, the influence of imitation and makes comparatively small allowance for spontaneous evolution and he does not expressly recognise the fact that imitation is in many cases founded upon Logic. This is notably so in the case of primi-

1 *Les Transformation de Droit* translated, in Kocourek and Wigmore, *Primitive and Ancient Legal Institutions*, p. 46.

tive social institutions. Let us consider the ritual of marriage, for instance. The ritual of to-day is the result of a long course of evolution, in the course of which it has brought together a number of different rites and built them up into the complicated ceremony of to-day. In its origin, the ritual was probably founded upon the imitation of the words and acts of some one person. But why was that act or word imitated ? The reason was that primitive man believed very much in supernatural influences and the efficiency of magic in dealing with such influences.[1] When therefore a man successfully went through a transaction, whose nature people did not exactly understand, without incurring any one of its supposed dangers, his neighbours would place the credit of his success with something done by him or some words uttered by him. It is because they thought that his words and acts had such magic influence that they repeated them when they themselves wanted to go through the same dangerous transaction. If the trick succeeded in other cases, it became gradually established as a customary ritual. In these cases, therefore, the imitation is not imitation pure and simple, but imitation prompted by Logic. In point of fact it would be very difficult to conceive of cases of imitation which was conscious, without conceding some part in it to logic. In unconscious imitation, on the other hand, which forms a great part of the daily life of man, the element of logic is entirely absent.

Imitation or borrowing from the institutions of races and communities other than one's own is really an extension of this primary instinct of imitation. We must not suppose that ancient peoples were very prone to imitate from their neighbours. On the contrary they had a very strong sense of the sanctity of their own customs and usages and were hardly likely to give up their own customs in favour of a foreign one. But circumstances occur in which the choice is more or less forced on them. When a people find themselves placed in an environment for which their time-honoured laws and customs are not suited and social and economic needs press upon the community they are found to seek satisfaction of their necessities by following the example of their neighbours. It is not a very simple process.

1 Crawley, *The Mystic Rose*.

We do not know the exact circumstances under which any community got over its primary prejudice against customs and usages of alien races and adopted or adapted such foreign customs. Some very strong reasons of convenience must always have existed. But in very early times, mere convenience would hardly tell in favour of a custom unless it could be coupled somehow with argument from magic.

MAGIC AS A FACTOR IN THE EVOLUTION OF LAW : Magic has played a very important part in social evolution. It has led to developments in laws and institutions in a very startling manner. Ancient and retarded races conceive their lives to be surrounded by a considerable amount of danger from supernatural forces. Every important and unimportant act in this view might involve consequences that might prove serious, as a result of supernatural forces let loose by that act. But such evils might be counteracted by magic and there is a tendency to look upon every trifling act as having more or less magical influence. In this way there are developed in the course of time elaborate codes of ritual and ceremonial which embrace eventually every little act of every day life.

PRIMITIVE LOGIC AND MAGIC : Primitive logic was founded mostly upon this magic. When the thing was done for a particular purpose there was a tendency to attach a magical effect to it. The extension of the same magic to other similar institutions or acts was the chief function of this logic. Thus a particular act may have been originally prompted by a natural desire or some consideration of convenience. But a magic effect is attached to the act when it has become established in custom and people of a later day try to elaborate that magic and extend it to other similar acts in which there is neither the original motive nor any consideration of convenience.

CHAPTER III

PRIMITIVE AND ANCIENT SOCIAL ORGANISATION

Before we can expect to get anything like a complete idea of ancient laws it is necessary to have a correct notion of the society in which those laws existed. Social organisation is perhaps the most important factor in the history of ancient law.

PRIMITIVE SOCIETY RACIAL AS DISTINGUISHED FROM NATIONAL : Primitive society as distinguished from modern society is racial as opposed to national. Modern society is organised in states or political units of society which constitute nations. We might say that the modern national society is on the way to becoming international. And, already we may find in the organisation, for example, of the British Empire, consisting of so many countries and nations living wide apart from one another, a society which has out-stripped the limits of national organisation. But that is another story. As distinguished from societies of the past, modern society is national. The basis of communion between the members of modern society is—living in the same country, governed by the same political authority. On the contrary ancient social organisation did not take account of contiguity in space or community of allegiance but proceeded almost entirely on the basis of race, that is, descent from common ancestors, real or fictitious.

RACE IS FAMILY WRIT LARGE : The germ of the race therefore is to be found in the family and one might almost say that primitive society is family writ large.

GENS : From the family developed by a course of natural expansion the clan or *sippe* or *gens*. All these, as well as similar organisations based on matrilinear kinships[1] are only expan-

[1] Some Anthropologists are inclined to use the term 'clan' to signify matrilinear clans only. That can only lead to confusion of language. For no convention is likely to change the name of the clans of the Highlands.

sions of the family. The members of a clan are all supposed to be descended from a common ancestor and it is this tie of blood that constitutes relationship and racial and social affinity. One remarkable evidence of this circumstance is furnished by the fact that, in primitive society, all clansmen are called by their relational names and not by their proper ones.

TRANSITION FROM CLAN TO THE STATE : Maine supposes that the primitive or ancient state is in the same manner a result of the further expansion of the family. The family expands into the *gens*, the *gens* into the *tribe* and the *tribe* into the *state*, which in ancient times consists of men, all of whom are supposed to be descended from a common ancestor. This theory however is only partially correct. The tribal organisation and the organisation into states involves the operation of a principle different from that of common descent. That is military principle.[1] The tribe is the clan or group of clans organised for military purposes under the authority of a chieftain who becomes, later on, the king of the ancient state. The basis of the organisation is military necessity and convenience and, although the material for the organisation is furnished primarily by the clan, we find that military exigencies very often lead to the inclusion of non-clansmen within the tribal or the state organisation. Altogether there seems to be little doubt that, as pointed out by Ihering, while the clan or *gens* was developed by the natural expansion of the family, with the principle of cohesion furnished by kinship, the tribe and the state were moulded and given their form by the military principle. The chief of the tribe as well as the king of the primitive state is only the military captain and he owes his pre-eminence to his personal prowess and capacity for military organisation.

STATE IN PEACEFUL TIMES—THE KING AS JUDGE : When the state has outlived the period of external strife and continues in more or less peaceful times the organisation of society finds placed at its head a man who concentrates in his hands, in the highest degree, the physical strength in the state. There is now a tendency for all power in the state to gravitate towards

---

1 Ihering, *Geist der Romischen Rechts*, Vol. I, p. 245 *et seq*.

him. Military necessity makes it obligatory to impose restriction upon the liberty of individuals for the purpose of maintaining peace and order amongst the fighters. By reason of the necessity for maintaining peace and order within the state in times of peace, the king gradually becomes the judge. We find him the administrator of all affairs of the state. And as a person, he towers above every individual and every institution. It is in this way that the state is gradually established. Inspite of this, however, the tie which unites the different members of the state is supposed to be common descent. Men are not Romans or Athenians or Spartans by reason of their being born of the soil of Rome, Athens or Sparta, nor by reason of their habitual residence in those cities, but by reason of their actual or supposed descent from the founder or founders of the cities. These ancient states are therefore primarily aggregations of kinsmen or blood relations, qualified by the circumstance that many persons who were not of the kindred had been adopted into the society, either as individuals or by clans.

DUALITY IN PRIMITIVE STATES : In most places we find that as a result of this a duality grows up in the constitution of each ancient state. The Roman, that is, the Patrician, is the person who has the full status of the Roman citizen with the full rights both in private and in public Law (*cives optimo jure*). But we find that there is also a large population of persons who are not entitled to those privileges although they live in the city. The Plebeians, in early times, the Peregrins or the Dediticii were not, strictly speaking, members of the state. Similarly in India we find that the Aryans are the only classes who are supposed to constitute the state and in whom alone the Laws are interested ; while the *Sūdras*, and, still less, the *Antyajas*, who live in the same state, are not supposed to participate in the laws of institutions of the state. This condition of affairs arises from two classes of circumstances ; either the ruling class has come and settled down in a locality where the native population is immediately reduced to a position of subordination and, possibly, servitude ; or the inferior class have gradually come and settled in the city founded by the superior class either for support and protection or for purposes of trade or otherwise. When this subordinate population grows in importance and attempts to establish its rights on a footing of equality with the higher classes they can only take their stand upon a principle of social organisation, different from kinship, namely, local contiguity. The Plebeians of Rome asserted their rights in this way and laid the foundation for the development, in course of time, of local contiguity as the principle of social organisation. This principle, strengthened still further by the sway of feudalism in Europe now holds the ground as the only principle of social organisation in civilised states. No doubt there is still a certain element of hereditary or racial connection in the organisation of men in a state. The Frenchman is not only the man who lives in France but one who is, generally speaking, descended from a Frenchman. As I have observed however, the principle of race as binding together the members of a state is gradually giving way before the wider conception of internationalism.

CHAPTER IV

FAMILY AND KINDRED[1]

FAMILY THE KERNEL OF ANCIENT SOCIETY: The family is the pivot of ancient society. The clan or *gens* and the other units of society are expansions of or organisations growing out of the family. The nature of the social organisations depends, in a very great measure, upon the character and the organisation of the family. Besides, almost everywhere in a primitive society we find that the family is an *imperium in imperio*—a sort of miniature state within the state. The head of the family, whoever he is, is the absolute master in respect of affairs which concern the family alone, the state interfering only in affairs affecting different families. In Rome this authority of the head of the family was manifested in a superlative form. The head of the family, the husband or householder is the absolute master over his wife and children under *potestas* and over his slaves, so much so, that he has the *jus vitae et nescis* and complete power over the properties acquired by the members of the family. There are scholars who look upon this as the result of a line of development from the primitive father-right which, according to them, was not so exaggerated in its earliest form. But elsewhere also we havet his *jus vitae et nescis* and the property of the father over the acquisitions of wives, children and slaves.[2] It is quite clear that, at any rate amongst most, if not all, ancient and primitive societies the family was the final authority in deciding disputes between members of the family and anything happening within the family, which did not affect any other family, was a purely domestic matter in which the authorities of the State have no right of interference.

---

1 Read Maine, *Ancient Law*, Chapter V.

2 In Hindu Law for instance Vasistha speaks of the parents having the right to sell, give or mortgage sons. Sunahsepa is sold by his father to be sacrificed. In most countries the father had the right to expose the child—notably the female child.—Vinogradoff, *Historical Jurisprudence*, p. 234.

CLASSES OF FAMILIES—PATRIARCHAL : We shall therefore discuss the constitution and organisation of the family in ancient and primitive systems of Law. With regard to organisation, families may be divided into three classes, the Patriarchal and the so-called Matriarchal and the Totemic families. In the first, the headship belongs to the father and it consists of the father, his wife or wives and the descendants of the husband and wife. This family expands along the lines of agnatic kinship ; or, in others words, kinship is counted through males only and not through females. The *gens* which develops out of this family is a group of families or kindred who are related to one another through males alone. Maine points out that the foundation for this agnation or relationship through males is to be found in the *Patria Potestas* so that the agnates are those relations who would have lived under the same paternal authority or within the same family organisation if their common ancestor had been alive.

MATRIARCHAL FAMILY : The so-called Matriarchal families on the other hand are groups which form round the mother. The stock of the family is the mother and the family consists of sons and daughters of the mother and sons and daughters of the daughters. The sons and daughters of the males of the family have no place in a strictly matrilinear system. The women do not go and live with their husbands in the husband's house. They live with the mother even when they are mated and the children to whom they give birth are members of the mother's family. In a society of this character the development of the wider groups naturally takes place along the lines of matrilinear kinship ; that is to say, people are considered as related to one another who are descended from a common female ancestor through females only. The son or daughter of a male member of the family is not a member of the family, because his mother lives in her mother's house and only receives her husbands there ; and the children would be born in their mother's family. In most cases, however, we find that the family is not matriarchal, strictly speaking, because the stock of the family, the mother, though she usually holds a position of greater honour and authority in the family than a patriarchal *materfamilias*, is not the real head of the family. The headship very generally belongs to her brother or nearest male kindred. But the family is matricentric and the kinship which arises out of this family organisation is matrilinear.[1]

DIFFERENCES FOUNDED ON DIFFERENT VIEWS OF MARITAL RELATIONS : The root of the difference between the two systems consists in the different ideas with regard to marital relations. In the patriarchal society marriage is considered as a union more or less permanent, between one male and one or more females, with the result that the woman is taken out of her father's family and authority and comes under the authority of the husband. Marital union in the matriarchal family on the other hand consists of a relationship between men and women which involves no change of kindred on the part of the woman, no change of the authority over her and hardly any outstanding obligations between the man and the woman such as we have in the patriarchal society. Such marital union may be polyandrous or monandrous. Of the polyandrous form we have an illustration amongst the Nairs of Malabar ; of the monandrous, the typical illustration is to be found in the *beena* type of marriage.[2] In the patriarchal marriage there is always

1 In most matrilinear societies this strict scheme of kinship has been more or less modified by the inclusion of the children of males in the kindred. They are families therefore of a mixed type, just as most actual instances of patriarchal societies show a more or less liberal admission of cognates to the kindred. The *beena* type of marriage prevailing in societies which are otherwise patriarchal is an indication of the mixing up of a patriarchal with a matriarchal institution. (Vinogradoff, *op. cit.*, p. 195).

2 *Beena*, properly speaking, is the name of a form of marriage prevalent amongst the Sinhalese in Ceylon. In it the daughter lives in the father's house where she is visited by her husband. Her children becomes her father's kinsmen. But the term *beena* marriage was extended by Morgan as a technical term to imply all marriages of this type in which the husband visited the wife and it has been used in that sense by others, notably by Robertson-Smith. (*Kinship and Marriage*, p. 87.). It is to be noted that this is not a purely matriarchal institution, for the kinship of the *beena* wife and her children is with her *father* and not her mother. It is obvious that this was a variant of the matriarchal form in which the daughter would live with her *mother* and be kindred to her mother's kin. This type of marriage finds its analogues in the *Mahabharata* stories of the marriage of Arjuna with Ulupi and Chitrangada.

involved, in a more or less pronounced form, the idea of ownership or authority over the wife and it is this notion of authority which sticks to the relation to the last. It is entirely different with marital relationship in matriarchal societies.

THEORY OF THE EVOLUTION OF PATRIARCHAL MARRIAGE FROM PROMISCUITY : Since the middle of the last century the question as to the relative position of these two types of marital union and family organisation, in the order of evolution of society has been the subject of acute controversy between different schools of sociologists and legal historians. A school of thinkers including McLennan, Morgan, Fustel de Coulanges, Kohler and others have maintained that the matricentric family is the prior of the two types of family organisations. Before the proprietary or patriarchal form of marriage was evolved, the marital union took place on the lines of polyandrous union of the Nair society which also was preceded, according to most of these writers by group marriage and promiscuity. In other words, humanity in its origin, knew nothing of any marriage bonds. Men and women had intercourse just as they pleased, without any restriction whatsoever. Gradually however the notion of temporary appropriation grew up, as sexual jealousy came in. In the effort to appropriate the women to themselves, men built up the proprietary form of marriage. So long as the sexual relations were promiscuous, and also during the period of qualified promiscuity, children naturally grouped round their mother ; and thus the family organisation belonging to this stage of society is naturally matriarchal. On the contrary, when the woman became the property of the man, the children of the woman, who were assets in primitive society, belonged by right to the owner of the woman. Thus, in this view, the partiarchal family with patrilinear kinship was a later growth.

MAINE'S THEORY OF THE PRIMACY OF THE PATRIARCHAL SOCIETY : On the contrary Maine insists that the primitive family was patriarchal, and of the type which is depicted in the *Old Testament* and in Homer's description of the Cyclops. From the evidence of the *Old Testament* and that of social institutions of Romans, Hindus and Slavonians as well as from Homer's description of Cyclopean society, Maine concludes that "the effect of the evidence derived from comparative jurisprudence is to establish that view of the primeval condition of the human race which is known as the patriarchal theory."[1] He thus summarises the character of that system : "Men are first seen distributed in perfectly isolated groups held together by obedience to the parent. Law is the parent's word."

NEITHER THE PATRIARCHAL NOR THE MATRIARCHAL—THE UNIVERSAL PRIMITIVE TYPE : The evidence which has been brought forward of the matriarchal theory from all parts of the world makes it impossible to insist that the patriarchal society was the only possible type of primitive society. At the same time the theories put forward by those who insist on promiscuity followed by mother-right as the primitive type from which the patriarchal society was developed later on, cannot be sustained. As Westermarck[2] points out, there is no trace of the actual existence of promiscuity as a principle anywhere and at any time ; it does not even exist in the animal world among the higher mammals ; and amongst the apes, the hordes with the male as its leading member is already an established fact. Sexual jealousy finds its full play among the higher animals. It is not likely therefore that a condition of promiscuity could have been tolerated by the primitive man. The evidences which have been brought forward in favour of the theory of promiscuity are chiefly, not cases of absolute promiscuity, but what are known as group marriages, which are of various kinds ; and, in many cases, these group marriages represent not so much actual marriages between groups as the range of possible marriage.[3]

FORM OF MARRIAGE AND SOCIAL ORGANISATION MOULDED BY ENVIRONMENTS : As the evidence now stands, it is not possible to say with any assurance either that primitive society was everywhere of the patriarchal type or that one type was derived from the other. Although we cannot thus go to the root of social institutions, we can notice that the form of social organisation everywhere is to some extent moulded by social and economic environments. The relative numbers of the two

1 Maine, *Ancient Law*.

2 *History of Marriage*, 3rd Ed.

3 Vinogradoff, *Historical Jurisprudence*, Vol. 1, p. 184.

sexes, the physical and social surroundings of the community, the pressure of external enemies and such other circumstances are often found to make a particular form of social organisation the most suitable for the community. Thus where a community is constantly engaged in warfare, the males constantly have to live away from home, and women are left to themselves, mother-right finds a hospitable soil. Similarly, as illustrated in the case of the Nambudri Brahmins of Malabar, the paucity of females coupled with residence amongst a polyandrous community accounts for the adoption of polyandry and matriarchaic by a people. The Nambudri Brahmins are undoubtedly of Aryan descent and the existence of patriarchal institutions amongst them is evidenced by the fact that the eldest son of a Nambudri always marries according to the *Arya* rite. The younger sons however have *Sambandhams* like all the other classes of people in Malabar. This was due to the fact that unless this was allowed, marriage would be an impossibility in the case of most Brahmins in the Malabar.

THERE MAY NOT HAVE BEEN ONE PRIMITIVE TYPE : The contention therefore seems to be justified that the particular form of family organisation and marriage which we find in vogue in any community is the result of the pressure of environments. Under the pressure of one set of facts a particular society develops patriarchal institutions and patriarchal marriage. Under another set of circumstances another particular community develops matriarchal institutions. The possibilities of different forms of sexual union are not unlimited and may be looked upon as practically limited by the actual forms which we can study amongst ancient and primitive as well as modern races, including retarded races. Primitive man in different environments, under the pressure of different sets of circumstances adopted one or the other of these limited number of possibilities. The result was the formation of different types of society and social institutions some of which were patriarchal and others were matriarchal, some of which were monogamous and others were polygamous. It is not necessary to assume that all these variations must have proceeded from any common root or that any one of these forms must be looked upon as the primitive type from which the other forms may have been derived.

MARRIAGE RULES EVOLVE OUT OF PRIMITIVE TABOOS : The intercourse between man and woman is, as we have seen, nowhere absolutely free and unrestricted. Amongst the savage races there are wide ranges of taboo excluding the possibility of intercourse between man and woman. It is only within a certain range of relations that intercourse is permissible and then only under more or less severe regulations. These marital relations are therefore regulated or placed under a system even amongst the most backward races, although there are races which permit polyandry and polygyny and even group marriages approaching promiscuity. It is out of these regulations of marital relationships in primitive society that the institution of marriage has arisen.

DIFFERENCES IN TYPES OF FAMILIES DUE TO DIFFERENCES IN MARRIAGE FORM : I have drawn attention to the distinction between the two principal types of marital relations. In the matriarchal society, whether polyandrous or otherwise, marriage creates comparatively few outstanding obligations as husband and wife. There are no obligations of the husbands nor any rights in respect of the children. In some such societies, as amongst some of the Bedouins, the husband and wife have a tent to themselves, in which they carry on a sort of a household. But generally speaking, the husband is more or less like a visitor and he certainly has no authority over the wife. This means that the wife has generally a greater measure of freedom in such societies than in patriarchal societies. But this does not necessarily imply that the woman is free from all control whatsoever. She is under control of her mother's kindred and generally, her mother's brother or her own brother and the control is sometimes quite as great as that of the husband or father in a patriarchal family. In the patriarchal society, on the other hand, the effect of marriage is profound. Generally speaking there is everywhere, in such societies, the idea of the appropriation of a woman, that is the making of the woman into one's own property. The woman, generally obtained from outside the family circle, is made into the exclusive property of the husband who, if not precisely entitled to excluisve intercourse with the woman, was, at any rate, entitled to regulate the entire life of the woman, including her relations with other men. This notion of property, or, to be more precise, authority over woman lies at the root of the entire marital relationship in patriarchal society where the husband becomes the master and is entitled to deal with the woman more or less as he is entitled to deal with his cattle or slaves. In the patriarchal society therefore marriage is always marriage of dominion and it always leads to the acquisition of an amount of authority over children, who are looked upon more or less as a property of the father. Even in patriarchal societies there is a possibility not only for polygamy but also polyandry as in Tibet.

MARRIAGE THE FOUNDATION OF FAMILY AND KINSHIP IN PATRIARCHAL SOCIETY : This marital relationship, maturing in course of time into marriage, lays the foundation for the family in patriarchal societies and lays down the lines along which kinship develops. On the contrary, kinship in matrilinear societies is independent of marital relations altogether. Patriarchal kinship is an expansion of the family ; the kindred consist of those persons who would have been members of the family had their common ancestor been alive ; the root of the family lies in the marriage relationship.

MATRILINEAR KINSHIP BASED ON COMMON MOTHER : The two systems of kinship therefore may be distinguished as the natural and the legal. In matrilinear kinship the relationship is based upon the physical fact of a common origin in the mother's womb, which is an obvious fact, while fatherhood which forms the foundation of the other sort of kinship is not an obvious natural fact nor perhaps known in very primitive society. In the primitive patriarchal societies the element of fatherhood need not have been readily recognised either. A man was the owner of the wife and therefore the owner of all the offspring of the wife. The association of paternity with actual procreation might well have been recognised much later.

TOTEMIC KINSHIP : Apart from this Matrilinear and Patrilinear kinship founded upon motherhood and fatherhood respectively, there is yet a third form of kinship and that is the Totemic kinship, which, as Vinogradoff says, "is neither entirely agnatic nor entirely cognatic, being based neither on appropriation nor purely on the household, but on a religious system," and he quotes the following description by Mathews[1]. "In the Chau-an as well as in all the other tribes reported by me, in the Northern Territory, succession of the totems does not depend upon either the father or the mother, but is regulated by locality, and I shall now endeavour to describe how this is carried out. The folk-lore of these people is full of fabulous tales respecting the progenitors of every totem. Some of them were like the men and women of our own time, whilst others were mythologic creatures of aboriginal fairyland. In these olden days, as at present, the totemic ancestors consisted of families or groups of families, who had their recognised hunting-grounds in some part of the tribal territory. They were born in the specific locality, and occupied it by virtue of their birthright.

"In all aboriginal tribes there is a deeply seated belief in the re-incarnation of their ancestors. The original stock of spirits, so to speak, perpetually undergo re-incarnation from one human being to another. The natives are quite ignorant of the natural facts of procreation, and believe that conception is altogether independent of sexual intercourse. When a woman for the first time feels the movement of the child in the womb, commonly called quickening, she takes particular notice of the spot where it occurred and reports it to the people present. It is believed that the spirit or soul of some deceased progenitors has just at that moment entered the woman's body. The entry may have been by way of some one of the natural openings, or through any part of the skin, the mode or place of ingress being immaterial to these ethereal beings. When the child is born it will have assigned to it the totemic name of the mythic ancestor belonging to the particular locality."

SYNTHETIC KINSHIP OF MODERN CIVILISATION : Totemic connections belong now to only the most backward races of the world. Scholars have attempted to discover traces and survivals of totemism in the scheme of kinship of civilised races.[2] But leaving that apart, one may say that in civilised society the only

1. Quoted by Vinogradoff, *Historical Jurisprudence*, PP. 205 ff.

2. Thus Exogamy is considered to be a survival out of the Totemic notions of Kinship. (See Andrew Lang quoted in Kocourek and Wigmore, *Primitive and Ancient Legal Institutions*, P. 216.)

forms of kinship which may be said to have survived, are patrilinear and matrilinear. Generally speaking the scheme of kinship of civilised society consists now-a-days of a mixture of the two types or in a recognition of the claims of blood both through the father and through the mother. Civilised society has arrived at this synthetic form of kinship in very different ways in different societies. But everywhere in partiarchal societies the motive principle has been opposed to the authority of the father. As I have pointed out before, the agnatic kinship was based upon the fact of the family organisation being founded on a proprietary basis. Everywhere in civilised society this family of dominion gradually broke down and yielded place to the family, more or less of free association or a corporation. Along with this change the old idea of kinship founded upon this authority gradually yielded place to one of blood relationship, and once this was achieved, the blood of the mother gradually got into its own as a principle of almost equal efficacy with the blood of the father.

METHODS OF SYNTHESIS : But although this was the motive force behind the change which came sooner or later in the different patriarchal societies, the change itself was historically accomplished under widely varying circumstances. In Roman Law cognation was recognised as the principle of kinship under the influence of the doctrine of the Law of Nature and introduced into the Roman legal system by the Edict of the Prætor. In India the result appears to have been arrived at by a circuitous process. The transition from the purely agnatic kinship to the cognate kinship was effected through the instrumentality of the *Putrika* or the appointed daughter, who by a fiction of law was looked upon as a son and whose son also became son of the maternal grandfather and not of the father. We can see how, in the course of the history of Hindu Law, in time this institution of *Putrika* lost all formality and became transformed into the rule that daughter of a sonless man would practically take the place of the son. In other words the daughter's son became recognised as kindred through the intermediate stage of the fiction of *Putrika*.[1] The exten-

1. For a discussion of this proposition see an article in the *Man*, Vols. XXIV, pp. 32 and 42 by the present writer.

sion of the same principle of kinship to collaterals, who were all daughter's sons of some member of the family was only a question of time. It is possible that the model for the *Putrika* was obtained by the Aryan of India from neighbouring matriarchal races, or races with modified matriarchal institutions, though the motive force behind the change was supplied by natural affection conditioned by changed social environments.

The same result was apparently arrived at in other societies in other ways. Thus Vinogradoff points out that offensive and defensive alliances between tribes may have laid the foundation of cognation in many societies. The exigencies of warfare may have made such alliances useful and marriage has been known all over the world as a device for cementing such alliances. After such marriage the two tribes no longer remain strangers to one another, but become kinsmen with the same obligations in respect of helping the kinsmen against enemies as the agnates.

BREAK-UP OF PATRIARCHAL FAMILY AND SOCIETY : The recognition of cognation meant the break-up of the patriarchal family and society. The family which would now include daughter's sons would no longer be the family held together by the *Patria Potestas*. The kindred would no longer consist of agnates alone but would include a large body of families related through females. It would naturally embrace a wider society than the old patriarchal society, the association with gods and institutions of different previously isolated social groups all brought together by a new principle of association, *viz.*, blood-relationship and natural affection.

DECAY OF THE FAMILY : This widening of the society frequently bore in it the seeds of the decay of the old family, the *imperium in imperio* dominated by the absolute will of the house-father. We start with a stage of society in which the family is a unit of social organisation and in which the authority of the father is the only Law within the family, the state being concerned only with relations between families. In course of time we find this organisation breaking down under attacks from more than one direction. Thus, in the first place we find the state gradually making incursions into disputes between members of the family. In an early stage of Hindu

Law, Gautama says that, as between father and son, husband and wife and preceptor and pupil, no litigation is possible. In other words this means that the state has no jurisdiction in disputes between members of the family. That was also the law elsewhere in Aryan society. But, even in Gautama, this restriction had ceased to have legal validity and Gautama himself recognises and, as we go on to the later history of Hindus, we find it increasingly recognised, that litigation is possible between husband and wife, the father and son, over a variety of topics affecting their personal and proprietary relations. A similar process is discernible in other Aryan societies.

Patria potestas developed in families without adult children : Primitive Aryan society apparently consisted of families which had no adult children in it. All the indications in the *Vedas* taken along with the ritual literature point to the fact that early Aryan society consisted only of husband and wife and immature children.[1] Grown-up daughters were married into a different family and went out, and at an immature age. Children were sent out for instruction to the *Guru* with whom they lived till the instruction was completed. On coming back from the *Guru* the *Arya* got married and set up a house for himself, symbolised by the lighting of a sacred *Grihya* fire. Thus, grown-up sons also were not members of the father's household. In course of time however it seems that the grown-up son began to live with the father. This led to profound changes in the family Law.

Disintegration of patria potestas with the growth of large families : The family Law which gave to the father absolutely autocratic powers and *Jus vitae et nescis* belonged properly to the state of society in which the father lived with

1. The text of the *Rig Veda*, X, 85, 46 ; सम्राज्ञीश्वशुरे भव, etc., Be mistress over the mother-in-law, ete., referred to by Vinogradoff, *op. cit.*, Vol. I, p. 262, does not indicate that the father-in-law, sister-in-law, etc., lived jointly with the husband. Although living in separate houses they formed a unit of society together. In the marriage ritual of the *Rig Veda*, X, 85, 33 and *Atharva Veda*, XIV, 38, 29 we find these relations coming to bless the new bride and then apparently going away. For a more detailed consideration of the joint family in ancient India, see Appendix.

only very young children. It was obviously unsuitable to the family of adult children and grand-children and great-grand-children perhaps. The anomaly of these powers could not but be felt in such a family. The result was a reaction which led to substantial changes in the family Law in the course of time. In Rome the law relating to the power of the father was not substantially altered, but we find that emancipation of sons has become a favourite in Roman society, quite early in their history. Besides the custom of giving *Peculium*, with practical independence, to sons largely obviated the necessity of alteration in the family Law. The alteration did come however and it was represented by the recognition of the son's property right in *Castrense* and *Quasi-Castrense Peculium*. That was as far as Roman Law actually went.

(1) SEPARATION OF SONS : In India the introduction of adult sons led to a three-fold development of the family Law. The elaborate treatment of partition of the family property among sons during the lifetime of the father which we find traceable so far back as the time of the *Veda*[1] indicated that such partition was fairly common when once the grown-up son became a member of the family.

(2) SEPARATE PROPERTIES OF SONS : In the second place we find the son's right to separate self-acquired property becoming gradually recognised in early law. The gains of war such as (*Sauryyadhanam*), the gains of learning (*Vidyâdhanam*), the property of the wife (*Bhâryyâdhanam*), and the affectionate presents made by the father (*Pitriprasâda*) are the first to be looked upon as the exclusive property of sons. In course of time however we find other items of self-acquired property being regarded as the property of sons over which the father had no right of ownership, till ultimately the general principle is enunciated that whatever is acquired by a person by his own

1. In the tradition of *Manu* dividing his property among his sons. *Taittiriya Samhita*, III, 1, 9, 4, cited in *Apastamba*, *Dharma Sutras*, II, 14, II. Such partitions were originally permissible only at the will of the father. Already in *Gautama* however, we find it stated that sons did sometimes as a matter of fact compel unwilling fathers to partition the property, though this is referred to as an impious act. *Gautama Dharma Sutra*, XV, 19.

efforts without detriment to the family property belongs exclusively to the acquirer.[1]

(3) DEVELOPMENT OF SON'S CO-OWNERSHIP IN FATHER'S PROPERTY : A third and more important way in which an inroad was made into the father's powers was the development of the rights of sons in the joint family property. In the earliest stratum of the law we find the father as the master of the property in his hands. Then, apparently with the introduction of the adult sons, we find moral restraints introduced to prevent the alienation of such property by the father to the detriment of the sons. In other words the immovable property was coming to be recognised as a fund for the maintenance of the family which the father had no power to dispose of just as he chose without the consent of his sons. At a still later stage we find this developing into the notion of restriction of the ownership of sons in the property in the hands of the father. This rule we find imposed in the later texts. This aspect of the law is found still more developed and emphasised in the commentaries and *Nibandhas* and established in custom as the equal ownership of the father and sons in ancestral, as well as self-acquired immovable property in the hands of the father. In other words, the family is changed in constitution from an autocratic body into a corporation of persons with equal rights. A somewhat similar movement of the family Law towards joint ownership is to be found amongst the Germanic races whose allod partook of the character of the Hindu joint family property. Similar institutions are also to be found amongst Germanic and Slavonian races.[2] I am disposed to look upon these similarities as independent developments under the pressure of identical forces rather than as evolution out of a common stock ; because in Hindu legal history the existence of an original stage of joint ownership is negatived by the Vedic Literature.

1. *Yajnavalkya*, II, 118 ; *Manu*, IX, 208.

2. See Vinogradoff, *op. cit.*, Vol. 1, p. 268 *et seg.* The existenee of similar institutions among Germanic races, including Anglo-Saxons is asserted by Seebohm *Auglo-Saxon Village Cmmunities* and *Tribal Custom in Anglo-Saxon Law*. Pollock and Maitland however altogether discredit the theory of the original communion of Germanic races, *History of English Law*.

In many of the Western European races, notably in England this disintegration of the family has extended still further and has resulted in a return, though in a quite different shape, to the original idea of a family consisting of husband, wife and immature children.

POSITION OF THE WIFE : With respect to the wife we find her position of abject dependence in patriarchal society gradually becoming more and more tolerable by reason of various circumstances. Amongst the Aryan societies, before their separation, they appear to have developed the notion of a spiritual identity of husband and wife in the religious law. However that may be, we find that in the religious law, the *materfamilias* or the *Grihapatni* holds a position of very great honour and dignity, and throughout the history of Hindu and Roman Law, religion has always tended towards the improvement of the wife's status. But under the influence of different social factors the Aryan society, both in Rome and in India, had to rise to the rank of marriage institutions not founded upon the religious Law, such as the *Co-emtio* and *Usus* in Rome and the *Râkshasha, Paisâcha, Asura* and *Gândharva* forms of marriage, in India.

HUSBAND-RIGHT AS DOMINION : With the introduction of these forms of marriage, husband-right became an unmitigated dominion. For the women who now became wives in these ways had, in the eye of the religious law in the remote past, a status no better than that of slaves. The wife became, not only completely subject to the authority and control of the husband, but also a person who might be practically sold or given away.

RELAXATION OF HUSBAND'S AUTHORITY IN ROME : In course of time however both in Rome and in India the position of the wife was gradually improved. In Rome this was achieved by the introduction of the custom of marriage without *manus* which had the effect ultimately of giving Roman wives an amount of independence, and even license, which has not yet been paralleled elsewhere. In respect of their property, women still theoretically remained under the control of a male guardian. But, in point of fact, the control was practically non-existent. Even such control, as there was, was removed in some cases, by the *Lex Julia et Pappia-Poppoea* and by other devices.

IN INDIA : In India the position of women was never improved, to the same extent. They continued to be under subjection of the husband and in the absence of the husband, of the husband's relations throughout. But there the proprietary rights of women were enlarged, first by the recognition of their right of ownership in some specific kinds of property and later by their unrestricted right of ownership over all of their self-acquisitions. With regard to their personal liberty, they had throughout, to rely for protection upon the dictates of religious Law.

FROM STATUS TO CONTRACT : We notice thus, that on all sides, the old family was breaking down. The result of this process has been summarised by Maine in the statement that the advance of all progressive societies has been from Status to Contract. In other words in primitive patriarchal society every man or woman was born to a certain set of rights and obligations determined by his or her position in the family. In the economy of the state his or her position as an individual did not matter. The result of the progress has been the establishment of the right of the individual as such and the determination of his rights and obligations, very largely on the basis of contract or free agreement of parties.

This process in the result of numerous social forces which have determined the form and shape of the particular history in each country. But there can be little doubt that the most powerful force which stated and determined description of the ancient family was the expansion of the family by the inclusion of adult sons. This led to the growth of a condition in the family to which the old order of things founded on the autocratic sway of the male parent was not suited. The breakdown of the old order was then inevitable though the result was achieved by a gradual process in history.

CHAPTER V

MARRIAGE

I have dealt with some of the problems of comparative jurisprudence arising out of marriage. I shall now proceed to deal with the evolution of the institution of marriage in society as a whole.

MARITAL INSTITUTIONS DEVELOP OUT OF PRIMITIVE RESTRAINTS ON SEXUAL RELATIONS : Marriage or, to use a term which is more comprehensive, marital relationships, originate in the animal instinct of mating, but it only becomes a marital relation by reason of the regulation of the animal instinct. One might almost say that marriage laws are the sum-total of the rules restricting intercourse between man and woman.

PROMISCUITY AS PRIMITIVE TYPE OF MARITAL RELATION : Reference has already been made to different theories with regard to the evolution of institution of marriage. One school, represented by McLennan, Morgan, Fustel de Coulanges, Kohler and others, holds that the primitive state of man was one of unqualified promiscuity. The earliest attempt at the regulation of promiscuous relationship is represented by group-marriage, in which the young men of one particular clan are supposed to be married to the young women of another clan. It cannot be regarded as certain, that any such institution as the actual marriage of two groups, as distinguished from a combination of polygamy and polyandry has ever existed. What we do find in actual cases is rather a rule that the young men of a particular clan are entitled to have marital relations permanent or otherwise with young women of another particular clan. In some cases these are coupled with looseness of marital relations which give the impression that the marriage between two groups has actually taken place. According to the school to whom we are referring, however, this group-marriage is a necessary stage in the evolution of monogamous marriages through the intermediate stages of polyandry and marriages of the *Beena* type. The marriages of dominion are the result of sexual jealousy and a desire to appropriate women to one's own self, exclusively, which according to these authors is an instinct of much later growth.[1]

MARRIAGE OF DOMINION AS THE PRIMITIVE TYPE : On the other hand there are anthropologists including the great Darwin[2] and a long line of his successors amongst whom the name of Westermarck may be mentioned as one of the most notable in recent times, who insist that the patriarchal form of marriage, in which the man dominates over and exclusively possesses the woman, was an original type of marital relationship. It has been pointed out that sexual jealousy is an instinct which finds the fullest scope even amongst the higher mammals, most notably amongst the apes. The higher apes generally roam in hordes consisting of one male and a group of females ; other males are rigorously excluded from the horde and even the grown-up male offspring is turned out. On the other hand, Westermarck points out that promiscuity as an actual institution is not traceable in any part of the world, either ancient or modern.[3] The conclusion therefore is probable that primitive man established dominion over women and excluded other men from the horde. In course of time, however, the grown-up sons were permitted to live within the horde but a complete taboo was established as between them and the women of the father's family. In other words such sons were bound to find their mates outside the family. It was in this way that exogamy originated in society according to this theory.

CRITICAL ESTIMATE OF THESE THEORIES : It is not possible to arrive at any conclusion with regard to the priority of the types of marriage vouched for by these different authorities. They all proceed upon the basis of certain observed facts. Group-marriage is an institution which is found in various

1. The transition is generally supposed to be effected through marriage by capture. This thesis is expounded by Dargun, *Mutterrecht and Raubehe*, in *Untersuchungen zur Deutschen Staats-und Rechtsgeschiehte*, Part 16.

2. *Descent of Man*, 2nd Ed., Vol. II, p. 395.

3. Westermarck, *History of Marriage*, 3rd Ed. pp. 385-540.

shapes amongst the retarded races of the world. On the contrary even among such a completely uncivilised race as the Veddas we find strict monogamy established. The most backward of these races roam about the forests in couples and they do not associate with any other people except their infant offspring. Whether the one or the other represents the primitive type we are not in a position to say exactly.

RESTRICTIONS ON MARITAL RELATIONS IN PRIMITIVE SOCIETY : At the threshold of civilisation, however, we do not find unrestricted marital relations. On the contrary we find that intercourse between the sexes is strictly limited by an elaborate code of taboos and other limitations and restrictions, not only with regard to the persons between whom intercourse is possible, but also with regard to the times when they are permissible and the essential preliminaries of such intercourse. These restrictions are so far pronounced that Crawley was led to the conclusion that, far from there being a freedom of intercourse between man and woman in society, the primitive condition was one of complete antagonism between the sexes. He also supposes that in primitive society intercourse between the sexes is considered to be a very dangerous act and all the resources of magic have to be utilised for the purpose of averting the danger of such intercourse. In the effort of the primitive man to avert these dangers an elaborate code of rituals and rules of exclusions and other restrictions are developed in course of time.[1]

It is not necessary for us to agree to the conclusions of Crawley with regard to sex antagonism and the danger of sexual intercourse in their entirety. It is unquestionable however that in primitive society everywhere we find intercourse between men and women hedged in by a number of restrictions with regard to the time, the place, the occasion and the relationship between the parties. These restrictions are very extensive in some societies and they are more limited in others. There are societies, no doubt, in which practically the only restriction with regard to relationship amounts to an exclusion of mothers and mothers-in-law, even marriages between brothers

1. **Crawley**, *The Mystic Rose*, p. 222 *seq.*

and sisters being permitted ; this can easily be explained by the pressure of other circumstances and ideas not necessarily appertaining to the primitive state of society. Primitive society everywhere appears to have had a more or less elaborate code of restrictions.

MARRIAGE LAWS EVOLVED OUT OF TABOOS : The marriage laws of the various societies are evolved out of these various restrictions. Thus, for instance, the institution of exogamy which compels a man to seek his mate from outside his own clan, originated in these primitive taboos. This institution has been differently explained by the different schools of anthropologists as referred to, before.

ORIGIN OF EXOGAMY : According to Kohler, for instance, exogamy arose out of the necessity for alliance between different clans. So soon as human society stepped out of its primitive barbarism, it felt the necessity for a combination or alliance of clans for defensive and offensive purposes. The absolutely primitive conditions of society must be assumed to be one of antagonism or conflict between clans ; there was no basis on which different clans could co-operate. When the necessity for co-operation with clans for defensive and offensive purposes was felt, there were only two different ways in which clans might come together. One was the assumption of a common origin, and the other, an offensive and defensive alliance on the basis of matrimonial relationship. The first method is illustrated by many ancient societies in which we find a basis for co-operation established on the fiction of common origin. Thus the Romans obviously absorbed some of the tribes which were not of the same race with them, but who were assumed to have been descended from the same ancestors. Sometimes the performance of a ceremony is believed to cause an artificial affiliation by reason of which, persons, notoriously not descended from a common ancestor, are grafted into the family stock. And once the people were incorporated into the tribe or clan, the obligation of help in offensive and defensive affairs became a religious duty on every clansman or tribesman. But the same result followed when different clans which did not believe themselves to be descended from a common ancestor entered into an offensive and defensive alliance and the most usual method of sealing such alliances was to arrange so that the youths of the two clans should intermarry. In other words, that no youth of a clan 'A' should marry within the same clan but should have marital relations with women of clan 'B' and *vice versa*—that is the two clans should be exogamous but limited in respect of marital relationship to the two clans only. By reason of such alliances exogamy was established, side by side with a limitation of the possibility of marital relationship to only a certain number of clans or groups. On the other hand, Darwin, Atkinson and others explain the origin of exogamy by supposing, as I have mentioned before, that the adult son was permitted to live in the family only on the understanding that he must seek his mate outside the family.[1]

ENDOGAMY : However exogamy may have been established, we find that it is an institution which is almost universal in the earlier stages of the evolution of society. Endogamy, on the other hand, which permits or compels marital relationship between members of the family, is always found to be due to the pressure of circumstances. Either it is the paucity of females, the difficulty of procuring brides from outside, or the reluctance to part with property to which the girl may be entitled or some other circumstance that lies behind the phenomenon of strict endogamy wherever it is prevalent.

The rules of exogamy, however, tend to grow less stringent in the course of time and, following the line of the evolution, determined more or less by the pressure of social environment, they lead on to the rules relating to prohibited degrees in marriage.

FORMS OF MARRIAGE : The forms of marriage are also traceable to their origin in the primitive taboos. In all pimitive societies marital relationship is permissible only with a certain number of preliminary rituals. This is accounted for by the belief that a number of evil influences are at work

1. Vinogradoff, *op cit.*, Vol. 1, pp. 180 ff., assigns three possible motives for the institution of exogamy : (*i*) attraction of the unfamiliar, (*ii*) the necessity of preventing strife within the family, and (*iii*) the uncertainty of fatherhood in primitive societies.

which might make the connection dangerous. The rituals therefore very often partake of the character of charms or magic for the purpose of averting these evil influences and for propitiating the helpful spirits or gods and securing their assistance. In addition to these there are some other circumstances associated with the act, specially amongst exogamous societies. The bride has to be procured and made one's own. This is done by some transactions by which ownership over the bride is fixed. The ceremonies by which this was achieved lead us back to a state of society in which they represented earnest realities.

The principal methods by which a bride could be obtained in primitive society are classified by Hobhouse under four heads ; Capture, Purchase, Service and Consent.

MODES OF ACQUISITION OF BRIDE : Attempts have been made by some writers to place the entire series of marriage forms in an evolutionary order. It is supposed by some that the earliest form of patriarchal marriage was marriage by capture, which was gradually replaced by marriage by purchase, the price of the bride being the recompense for the loss of the girl to the father. Still later, this was superseded by marriage by free consent. The other forms of marriage are supposed to be simply variants of these three forms.

CIRCUMSTANCES AFFECTING EVOLUTION OF FORMS : It is quite clear, however, that you cannot construct a single order of evolution in which you could place all the various marriage forms which we find anywhere. The form which marriage takes, is dictated very largely by a great many social circumstances. Under the pressure of a strict rule of exogamy, a community which finds itself placed amidst hostile tribes could not but have recourse to capture as a mode of acquisition of brides. In communities where marriageable girls are plentiful, purchase would necessarily be regarded as out of question and, rather than girls being sold at the importunity of the man, the solicitation would come from the girl's father. So also, where adult marriage prevails, the element of choice on the part of the girl herself will sooner or later assert itself and break through rules and forms which would coerce her will.

MARRIAGE FORMS IN ANCIENT INDIA : It is obvious that there have been societies which have lapsed from a more advanced form of marriage to a more primitive one. On the contrary there have been societies in which brides who were originally purchased or acquired by service to the father were, latter on, given away free. An instructive lesson on the question of the evolution of marriage forms may be obtained from a study of the marriage law of the Hindus. The most ancient form of marriage in India, as well as in other Aryan communities was the religious form, which is embodied, for instance, in the *Grihya Sutras*. The idea underlying the rituals is that there is an agreement between the bridegroom and the bride's father and that the bride is also a consenting party to the marriage. We notice further, that, far from the bridegroom being a humble suitor seeking a girl, he is an honoured guest who has been invited for the purpose of taking the girl, as a favour. The relationship which is created by the marriage is one of complete spiritual partnership. At a later date we find that the Aryan society in India adopted other forms of marriage, such as the *Rakshasa*, in which the bride is obtained by force of arms, *Asura* in which the bride is obtained by purchase, *Gandharva* in which the bride is obtained by her own consent alone and lastly *Paisacha* in which a bride is practically obtained by theft or fraud. Similarly in Rome, we find that the older idea of marriage which we find embodied in the confarreation is replaced by a form which was perhaps a survival of marriage by purchase and another form which was practically a marriage by consent. The reasons underlying these changes are, clearly, that in the environments in which the Aryan society found itself placed, the older ideas could not survive the changed circumstances and required the adoption or adaptation of forms of marriage which were foreign to the original idea of the Aryan marriage but which prevailed amongst their new neighbours.

EVOLUTION OF FORMS DETERMINED BY ENVIRONMENT : It seems therefore that the forms of marriage are very largely dependent on environments and as these differ in different societies in their origin as well as their latter development, the actual forms of marriage have varied greatly both in their origin and in their latter growth. It is not therefore possible to construct a single course of evolution which will account for all the various forms of marriage.

I do not propose to discuss all the various forms of marriage which have been in vogue in human society in different countries and in different times. Men have always wanted marital relationship with women. So soon as they wanted women exclusively to themselves, the necessity for appropriate methods of acquiring such exclusive right developed. Where there are no rigorous rules of exogamy the end might be achieved by the consent of the bride's father or the consent of the bride herself, who being a member of the family or clan did not raise serious objections. Sometimes the consent has to be acquired for consideration. Where girls are valuable assets, they would not be parted with, unless the parents had a *quid pro quo*. There are several variants of this consideration paid for the bride. Sometimes the bride's price is fixed, as for instance, in the *Arsha* form of marriage among the Hindus. At other times it is a matter of negotiation, as in the *Asura* form of marriage. Another form of payment is to be found in the service rendered by the bridegroom to the bride's father, as is illustrated in the case of Jacob's marriage in the *Old Testament*. On the contrary, where girls are far from prized and are regarded, as in the Vedic society, as more or less of a nuisance to be got rid of by all possible means, it is the father of the bride who is anxious to induce the bridegroom to accept the girl, and the marriage takes the form of a free gift of the girl and very often with presents, more or less valuable, for the bridegroom and the bride. This is the mental attitude probably illustrated in the chief forms of religious marriage in ancient India, in all of which the bride's father is anxious to give away the bride with ornaments and presents to the bridegroom. The same result would also follow where girls are prized, where they may be given as presents, valued on account of their worth, to persons, held in high esteem (like the priest in the *Daiva* marriage) whom the ather wishes to please. This mentality we find depicted in many of the marriages narrated in the *Mahabharata*.

Where endogamy is strictly forbidden there might be groups of intermarrying races living in amity with one another, between whom marriage would be a perfectly peaceful transaction and would be entered into in one of the forms above mentioned. Where there is strict exogamy and a clan finds itself placed among more or less hostile races or, where the fancy of a young man leads him to seek a bride from a hostile community, marriage by capture would become the appropriate form of marriage. Cases of real marriage by capture in the past history as well as amongst savage or semi-savage races of the present day are well-known. But in many cases the fight has sunk to more or less of a formality or a fiction. It is, in many places, looked upon as a point of honour not to let the bridegroom take the bride without a show of fight, although, as a matter of fact the marriage has been pre-arranged. Customs also develop out of this, by which the bridegroom is required to show his prowess either by fight or otherwise, before a girl is given to him. Cases of such customs are found in the wedding of Sita in the *Ramayana* and of Draupadi in the *Mahabharata*.

In every society however, there is a tendency for the affection of the bride to assert itself in the matter of the choice of the bridegroom. Even amongst savage races who deny any scope to the choice of the girl in the matter of selection of the bridegroom it is often found that prohibited unions are effected by elopement and a bride can in most cases have the man of her choice if she is sufficiently insistent.[1] Wherever adult marriage prevails, therefore, there is a tendency for the choice of the girl to become an important determining factor in marriage. This is illustrated in the history of ancient India where at a comparatively early date, not only were marital relations often established by elopement, but the *Gandharva* form of marriage was favoured by some schools of law on account of its being founded on affection,[2] and *Swayamvara* was a well established institution from the days of the early traditions embodied in

1 Vinogradoff, *op. cit.*. Vol. 1, p, 210 ; also Westermarck, *op. cit* The *Mahabharata* stories of the elopement of Rukmini and Subhadra are evidences of such elopement in Ancient India.

2 Baudhayana says गान्धर्वश्चाप्येके प्रशंसन्ति स्नेहानुगतत्वात्— "Some praise the *Gandharva* marriage, because it founded on affection." *Baudhayana Dharma Sutra*: S. B. E., p. 207.

the *Mahabharata*. On the other hand, various motives may impel the parents not to permit a free scope to the choice of the daughter in the matter of marriage. It may be, that such choice prevents the father from getting an adequate bride-price. Or, it may be that the young brides are liable to get into scrapes or into unsuitable alliances which might bring down the honour of the family ; or there may be a real desire on the part of the father to protect the children against the rashness of youth in making an unsuitable choice. Wherever such tendencies predominate, we can notice a movement in favour of the marriage of girls before they attain the age of puberty. This tendency results sometimes in the institution of infant marriages between very little children.[1] In many other cases however, it is not actual marriage that takes place but only a betrothal which is matured into marriage by some ratificatory act when the girls attain puberty.

The *Paisacha* form of marriage referred to in Hindu Law is a somewhat remarkable case. According to Manu's description of this form of marriage it consists in the ravishment of the girl by the bridegroom while the girl is either asleep, intoxicated or otherwise out of her senses. According to the description given in the older texts of the *Aswalayana Grihya Sutra* however, it appears to be a marriage with a girl who has been procured by theft while her relations were sleeping or under the influence of intoxicants. In this form the *Paisacha* marriage is really nothing more than the theft of a girl, which is recognised almost to the same extent as marriage by capture, as a mode of acquisition of girls among backward races even to-day. But the form as defined by Manu is also intelligible amongst backward races. We find that when a woman has been ravished by another man the relations of the woman insist on the ravisher taking the woman. This is looked upon as a form of punishment of the ravisher.[2]

In all these various forms of marriage the idea is to acquire

1 In the *Vedas* adult marriage is contemplated. But as early as the *Grihyas* we find a *Nagnika* prescribed as the most suitable girl for marriage. *Nagnika* is a girl who is not yet ashamed to go about naked. (See *e.g.*, *Manava Grihya*, VIII, 3.)

2 *Cf.* Westermarck, *History of Human Marriage*, 3rd Ed., p. 383 *seq.*

dominion or control over the woman. Slowly however the recognition of the personality of the woman asserts itself and marriage comes to be looked upon more and more as a partnership by mutual consent between the husband and the wife for the greater happiness of both. This tendency leads to the position of women as it survives and as it promises to be in the future. But we must not forget that every form of marriage that there has been has had its relative validity with reference to its own times and particular environments.

CHAPTER VI

SONSHIP

PATERNITY PROBABLY UNRECOGNISED IN PRIMITIVE TIMES : The concept of paternity is by no means an absolutely primitive one. The relation of the son to the mother is an obvious natural fact and it is still further emphasised by the association between the mother and child during the prolonged period of nurture and upbringing of the child. The relations between the mother and the child therefore meet us on the threshold of the history of human society. Paternity however is a more difficult concept. In its mature form it is based upon a recognition of procreation as a natural fact. The existence of backward races, however, among whom the natural fact of fatherhood is unknown, indicates that realisation of the natural relation between father and son was a comparatively late acquisition of humanity.

COUVADE : The first step towards the recognition of paternity is perhaps indicated by the curious ceremonies known among some savage races, which have been called couvade. It is found in various forms, but the essential idea in it is that the father has to pretend to lie in with the child after it is born. By this fictitious lying in, a relationship is supposed to be established between the father and the child. And this relationship was apparently unconnected with the fact of procreation.

PROPRIETARY CONCEPT OF SONSHIP : Among some races apparently, sonship was identified with the notion of dominion. All children over whom a person exercises father-right are his children. That would be the natural concept amongst the polyandrous races of the Tibetan type where natural paternity would be indeterminate, but all the brothers who have the same wife would be fathers of all the children of the woman. The analogies which we actually find employed to justify the concept are those of the produce of one's field or the increase of one's cattle. The children of one's own woman are one's own on the basis of the proprietary right over the woman.

PATERNITY ESTABLISHED OVER OTHER PEOPLE'S CHILDREN : By an extension of the argument underlying this sort of paternity, father-right, could be established over other people's children also. We find quite early in history that father-right can be sold, given away or acquired ; that is, as soon as father-right is conceived as ownership and ownership is conceived as capable of transfer. Father-right is now found to be acquired in ways in which ownership can be acquired.

CONSEQUENCES OF THE RECOGNITION OF NATURAL FATHERHOOD : The recognition of natural fatherhood is a fact of far different import. This is always associated with the fostering of the child by the father and the mother together and the establishment of relations of tenderness which is absent in the proprietary notion of fatherhood. It represents a very great advance in civilisation and culture and, in its earlier stages, it is inconsistent with the existence of artificial fatherhood of the other type. Once paternity is conceived as consisting in procreation, naturally the son begotten by oneself on one's wife would stand in a category apart.

NATURAL PATERNITY ESTABLISHED IN EARLY ARYAN SOCIETY : A study of the institutions of Aryan societies leaves no doubt that the early Aryan culture groups had already developed this idea of paternity. We may also infer that the fact of fictitious or artificial paternity was unknown to them. This conclusion appears to be suggested by the absence of any common name for the institution of artificial sonship in the various Aryan languages, although the institution of adoption appears to have been almost universal amongst ancient Aryan races. It is also further strengthened by the fact that during a fairly long period of their history in India the Aryans did not recognise any secondary sons.

SONSHIP IN THE RIG-VEDA : In the *Rig Veda* the son is found to occupy a high place in the affections of fathers and his religious importance is also conceived to be very great. But the *Vedas* throughout conceive the son begotten on one's wife as the only possible form of son and no secondary sons are thought of.[1]

The entire ritual literature of the *Srauta* and *Grihya Sutras* moreover confirm this view, inasmuch as there is no ceremony in that literature appropriate to the affiliation of a son. The significance of this important omission will be clear when we remember that every important event of the everyday life of the *Arya* as well as each determining incident of a man's life is provided with an appropriate ritual in the *Srauta* and *Grihya Sutras*.

TRANSITION TO SECONDARY SONSHIP : It is often too readily assumed that the passage from the legitimate son to the adopted son is more or less immediate. For, we find the institution of adoption in most peoples in some form or other. Fustel de Coulanges suggests that the transition was effected through the desire for perpetuating the family *sacra*.

Although the secondary or artificial son is a fairly widespread institution, it would be wrong to suppose that the transition was directly from natural paternity to the fictitious paternity by adoption. From what I have said it is clear that the recognition of natural paternity existed in Aryan society before fictitious paternity was recognised by them and paternity of the proprietary type, without reference to natural fatherhood, had died out, if it ever existed among them. The recognition of fictitious paternity came gradually, and adoption was not the earliest form in which it was recognised, at any rate in India.

EARLY FORMS OF ARTIFICIAL SONSHIP—FOSTERAGE : Artificial relationships are known to have been established in many places by other means than adoption. Kohler mentions two important modes : fosterage and blood fraternity. When a child is brought up by a person not its parent a relationship is established between it and its foster parents and their relations, which is largely akin to those of blood relationship. There is no fiction in this case. The bond of affection is in this case

---

1 Nicht soll man glauben, er konne durch Adoption ersetzt werden, denu "was von einen andern gezeugt ist keine (rechte) Nach-Kommenschaft." Zimmer, *op. cit.*, p. 318, *Rig Veda*, VII, 4, 7-8.

quite real and the legal relations which are established are merely analogical extensions of natural kinship.

BLOOD-FRATERNITY : Blood-fraternity on the contrary arises from a circumstance familiar to primitive and ancient societies. Two persons who want to become blood-brothers taste each other's blood. This is supposed, according to primitive conceptions, to create a complete identity of being between the two. The act of eating and becoming one with the thing eaten are associated together in primitive thought in numerous conceptions.[1]

These are the more familiar modes of creating artificial relationships in primitive and retarded societies. On the contrary, adoption or the making of another's son one's own where the idea of natural paternity is already developed, involves the taking of an intermediate stage—the recognition of property in sons.

EVOLUTION OF ADOPTED SON IN INDIA : In a sense, as I have said before, this is a more primitive idea than the recognition of natural paternity. But the recognition of natural fatherhood seems to result in the elimination of the primitive notion. At least, that is what we find in ancient Aryan society. Aryan society, placed amidst peoples with a different civilisation, appropriated, and possibly re-appropriated, the idea of ownership in sons and with it the concept of secondary sonship by purchase, adoption, etc. The mere fact that sonship by adoption is common to Rome and India does not in this case indicate a common origin of the institution.

The history of the evolution of secondary sons in ancient India is very instructive, as illustrating the very gradual stages by which the transition from procreative paternity to that of adoptive paternity may be effected. It is not suggested that the same course of evolution was followed everywhere. What it shows is that elsewhere also the transition may have been similarly gradual.

PRIORITY OF SONS BORN IN THE HOUSE OVER ADOPTED OR AFFILIATED SONS IN ANCIENT INDIA : I have mentioned already

1 This underlies the idea of sacrament and of eating the totem, and the *Purushamedha* sacrifice. (See R. S. Trivedi's *Yajna Katha* in Bengali.)

that the *Vedas* did not recognise secondary sons and the *Grihya* ritual is inconsistent with the existence of secondary sons. But so soon as we arrive at the stage of the *Dharma Sutras* we find not merely the son by adoption but twelve kinds of sons referred to. Now, in the earliest enumerations of secondary sons we find a primacy accorded to sons like *Putrikaputra*, or the son of the appointed daughter, the *Kshettraja* or the son of one's wife begotten by another, *Kanina*, or the son of one's maiden daughter and so on.

Sonship of adopted sons established through the proprietary idea : A consideration of the entire evidence relating to the evolution of sonship, leaves little doubt that the idea of these secondary sons were adopted by the *Aryas* in India from their non-*Arya* neighbours among whom not procreation, but ownership of the mother was the chief determining factor. Pressed by a crying need for male children perhaps, or from other social necessities, the *Aryas* adopted all these concepts and along with these the idea of sonship as essentially consisting in ownership. And, we find Vasistha in his *Dharma Sutra* basing the institution of adoption expressly on this fact of the father being the absolute master of the son, by virtue of his being the author of his being.[1]

The religious basis of adoption not primitive : Fustel de Coulanges exaggerates the importance of the religious element in adoption. The paternity was primarily due to the acquisition of ownership by transfer, the religious and social ceremonies were additions to the transaction made, because, to the Aryan, a religious ritual was an indispensable accompaniment of every important event of life. The nature of the ritual however is important. In Rome, as Fustel de Coulanges points out, some of the rituals appropriate to the birth of a child were performed at adoption. That indicates that the ceremony was improvised out of the ancient ritual law proper to natural sons. In India we have something similar to-day, but while the *Grihya Sutras* are wholly silent about rites of adoption, Vasistha in his description of the ceremony of adoption pres-

1 See on this subject my paper on Sonship in Ancient India in *Man*, Vol. XXIV, 32, 42.

cribes only a *homa* with the *vyahritis* which was a general sacrifice of auspicious effect performed on every conceivable occasion.

Far more important are the other provisions of Vasistha's text. He lays down that the king should be informed previously and all kinsmen invited to the ceremony. That signifies that a recognition of the son as a kinsman by the kinsmen of the father was necessary for adoption. The same thing we also find in the Aetleidung of the old Norse law.[1] The essential things in adoption therefore were, firstly the acquisition of authority by transfer of ownership and the recognition of kinship by the kindred. The genius of the Aryan race however soon overlaid the institution with rituals and also developed, apparently independently, in Rome and India, the notion that sonship is a spiritual relation created by the *sacra*. This idea underlies the speech of Cicero referred to by Fustel de Coulanges.[2] It is a quite familiar concept of the later legal literature of the Hindus. But that this was not the essential idea in an earlier age is indicated by the absence of any specific ritual calculated to create such occult consequences in the earliest texts on the subject.

1 Kohler, *Philosophy of Law*, p. 116.

2 Cicero *Pro Domo* 13, 14 quoted by Fustel de Coulanges, "To adopt is to seek by regular and sacred law that which by the ordinary process of nature he is no longer able to obtain."

CHAPTER VII

JUDICIAL PROCEDURE

ORIGIN OF JUDICIAL PROCEDURE IN PRIVATE REVENGE : Administration of justice or adjudication had, as has been already mentioned, a long history behind it. Some forms of ancient and primitive judicial procedure are known to us. From those might be inferred a course of history originating in private revenge and culminating in modern judicial procedure. Here, as well as elsewhere, we have got to bear in mind the warning, which I have already given, against attempting to construct a single universal course of evolution of legal remedies. There can be no doubt, however, that the foundation of the entire system of the administration of justice lies in the instinct of vengeance.[1] A person who feels himself injured seeks vengeance ; and a person who wants a thing to be done for himself by another tries to get it done, in either case by his own efforts, if possible. If he fails, or thinks he will fail, he seeks the assistance of his family and kindred.

BLOOD-FEUDS : In primitive society we find the kindred are all bound by the most drastic religious sanctions, to help their kinsmen in these feuds. A dispute between two persons therefore generally terminates in a fight, either between individuals or between families or clans or tribes. For a very long time in society this is found to continue as a normal and honourable mode of adjusting disputes. Blood-feuds are found to prevail in otherwise quite civilized communities.

INTERPOSITION OF COMMUNITIES : At some stage in the history of society however there is an interposition of communities for a settlement of disputes. This interposition takes different shapes in different communities, determined to a large extent by the peculiar condition of the community, their social organisation, the effectiveness of their sanctions and numerous other circumstances. Thus amongst some people, we

1 Holmes, *Common Law*, Lecture 1, *pp. 2 et seq.*

find disputes are settled by the entire tribal assembly,[1] among others they are taken to the king,[2] among yet others they are referred to the adjudication of specially sacred persons, whose decisions are looked upon as the decree of gods.[3]

THE KING'S INTERFERENCE : The study of the Roman *Legis Actio Sacramento* leaves an impression that the king first interposed between citizens in order to prevent an actual fight, and induced the parties to refer the matter in dispute to a person upon whom they had confidence. This may have been done by some primitive kings in order to maintain peace amongst the citizens among whom it had to be maintained, perhaps to prevent weakness in the ranks of the citizens in their wars against other races. The results were perhaps found satisfactory and other people who had disputes, wished to have the matter settled by the king. The king perhaps would not interfere or was not permitted to interfere in disputes except for the definite purpose of preventing a determined conflict between its citizens. Therefore, even if there was no armed conflict, the parties had to pretend to prepare to fight, in order to give the king the necessary opportunity and jurisdiction to interfere. A history somewhat like this perhaps lies at the back of the *Legis Actio Sacramento*, in which we find the real fight between parties reduced to a symbolism. Instead of fighting with a spear, the disputants pretend to do so with a wand and the Prætor who represents the king thereupon interferes. There is in the *Legis Actio Sacramento* no reference of the matter to an arbitrator chosen by the parties, but an appointment of a judge by the Prætor. But in the *litis contestatio*, a formality is gone through which keeps the appearance of the Judge being chosen freely by the disputing parties.[4] In this dramatic representation very probably survives the first interposition of the king in a dispute between Roman citizens in

1 *E. g.*, by the "Thing" of the Njaals Saga.

2 *E. g.*, in Greece of Homer, and Rome before the Republic. Latter, the Prætor stood in Rome in the place of the King.

3 *E. g.*, the *Parishads* in India or the star-gazers among the Kassites in Berosius's description.

4 Sohm, *Institutes of Roman Law* (Trans. Ledlie, 3rd Ed., p. 226).

ancient Rome. This is not the absolutely primitive idea of adjudication, at any rate, so far as any Aryan race is concerned.

EARLIER STAGES OF ADJUDICATION : Evidence among other Aryan races and also perhaps in some of the Roman institutions indicates an earlier stage in which such adjudication was done without interposition of the king, by clans or religious bodies. The *L. A. Sacramento* was therefore, really representative, not of the first act of adjudication in Rome but rather of the first interposition of the king in the adjudication of disputes. This is quite clear from a study of the institution of the Germanic and the Celtic races. In India the history will perhaps be found to be clearly recorded, if only we critically interrogate the legal documents that we have got. Such a study reveals to us that long before the king came to adjudicate on disputes between persons such disputes were quite peacefully decided by the intervention of the *Kulas* (family or clan assemblies), *Srenies* (Guilds of men following the same occupation) or *Parishads* (assemblies of learned men who knew the Law) and such other autonomous bodies.[1]

That in India also the interposition of the king in the decision of disputes was prompted by the same motives as in Rome, although not in the indentical manner perhaps, is indicated by the fact that in the earliest instances of disputes which are decided by kings, we find only thefts and offences of violence. It is only gradually that we proceed from this stage to that in which the king adjudicates on every kind of disputes. If we are in search therefore, of the absolutely primitive act of adjudication in Aryan society, we have to go behind the symbolism of the *Legis Actio Sacramento*. We can see that beyond this lies the adjudication of disputes by clans and guilds and religious societies.

JUSTICE IN PRIMITIVE SEMITIC SOCIETY : But the history of Aryan society leads us no further back. The study of primitive Semitic ociety gives us a glimpse at what was apparently a more primitive condition of things. The Law is thus summarised Cook :[2]

1 Sen-Gupta, *Sources of Law and Society in Ancient India*, pp. 18 *et. seq.*

2 *Laws of Moses and Hammurabi*, Extract in Kocourek and Wigmore, *Pr mitive and Ancient Legal Institutions*, pp. 655 *et seq.*

"Among primitive Semitic communities there is properly speaking, no law and law-givers. But it would be a mistake to infer that there was lawlessness. Tribal custom, and with it is involved religious custom, is the strongest of laws. A thing is lawful because it has always been considered lawful ; things that are unlawful are things that are not wont or ought not to be done. Within the tribe all men are on a footing of equality and under a communistic system, petty offences are unreasonable. Serious misdemeanour is punished by expulsion ; the offender is excluded from the protection of his kinsmen, and the penalty is sufficiently severe to prevent its being a common occurrence. The man who is wronged must take the first step in gaining redress, and when it happens that the whole tribe is aroused by the perpetration of any exceptionally serious crime, the offence is fundamentally regarded as a violation of the tribe's honour, rather than as a personal grievance on the part of the family of the sufferer. Courts, as in Babylonia, for the adequate punishment of offences and legally ordained punishments are not yet in existence. This essential distinction between primitive Semitic and Babylonian procedure comes out most clearly in the case of blood-revenge.

"The familiar Semitic conception of the sacredness of blood whether human or animal must have long been forgotten among the Babylonians, whose code is characterised by the frequent application of the death penalty. It is unnecessary to point out in detail how the Semites have been influenced by this conception. The inviolable nature of the blood-tie which makes kinsmen brothers and the responsibility attached to the shedding of blood, lie at the very root of the almost ineradicable system of blood-revenge. If a man has killed one of his own group he has committed an offence for which he cannot expect to obtain protection from the members of his tribe. He may be solemnly put to death and this was primarily effected without the spilling of blood, or he may be formally expelled, in which case he becomes an outlaw. In any case the community must be purged of the presence of the impious member. On the other hand, when the slayer and the slain are of distinct groups, the principle of the sacredness of blood reacts in a different manner. The group of the slain, on the one side, are bound in point of honour not to leave their kinsman's death unavenged ; the slayer's group, on the other, so far from being under an obligation to surrender the guilty one, regard it as equally a point of honour to unite to protect him. There is blood-feud between the two groups. Any member of the aggrieved group may retaliate upon any of the slayer's group, and until satisfaction is obtained, this state of feud continues. Naturally, under the circumstances, there may be indiscriminate slaughter, and the blood-feud is prolonged indefinitely. So deeply rooted is the practice that blood-revenge holds good among the wilder Bedouin tribes of to-day. Certain modifications, however, were gradually introduced with the object of preventing the fierce internecine fights and the insecurity of life which the feud entailed. Blood-wit was offered and accepted, the responsibility for murder was confined within limits, and retaliation restricted to the guilty party and immediate relations."

A study of the savage races of to-day and of the early laws of Germanic races,[1] gives further support to the conclusion that, everywhere, administration of civil justice originated in some similar manner. The person wronged seeks revenge, which, unless the wrong-doer is member of the community, he can always have with the assistance of his community who are pledged to support him. This naturally leads to the interposition of the communities as arbitrators in cases where both the parties are more or less amenable to the influence of the community. This arbitration may have come into existence in various forms and ways, but the motive behind it is everywhere the same, namely, to prevent, if possible, a blood-feud.

ADJUDICATION FOUNDED ON SELF-REDRESS : The most primitive adjudication of disputes seems to have taken the form of a decision on the question of the kind and quality of vengeance that the aggrieved person is entitled to get in justice.[2].

1. A good summary of the conclusions drawn chiefly from Germanic sources will be found in Vinogradoff, *op. cit.*, Vol. I, Ch. X.

2. Vinogradoff, *op. cit.*, Vol.I, p. 348, observes, "It may be said that an ancient trial was not much more than a formally regulated struggle between the parties in which the judges had to act more as umpire and wardens of order and fair play than as investigators of the truth."

That is why we find primitive law almost everywhere taking the shape of a tariff of damages to be paid for different kinds of wrongs. These damages represent an improvement upon the primitive measure of damages which is a measure of justified revenge. It is represented in the law of an "eye for an eye, a tooth for a tooth" or the *lex talionis* of the *Twelve Tables*. A later stage is reached when, instead of the wronged parties being permitted to take the revenge adjudged, the community adjudges the payment of a sum of money or other property as compensation for the injury done. This composition of wrongs was apparently a voluntary remedy which depended upon the choice of the wronged party. Later on however, it became the usual thing, and we find the composition is forced upon people by the conscience of the community and freedom of taking revenge is gradually taken away. This leads to the formation of elaborate tariffs of damages for various kinds of injury which we find in ancient laws as well as amongst retarded communities.

RELIGIOUS SANCTION OF THE LAW OF PROCEDURE: An important fact to notice about the early law of procedure is the religious sanction attached to it. The litigation is throughout, a religious process and is generally started by the taking of an oath by the parties. The man who lose a suit becomes an offender against the religious law for having taken the false oath. This is the idea underlying the *Legis Actio Sacramento*. The *sacramentum* was originally meant as a *pia mentum* or peace-offering to Gods to appease their wrath on account of their false oath.[1] Maine supposes this to have been the remuneration for the judge such as is indicated in the Homeric legend relating to the design on the shield of Achilles. This does not seem to be supported by the testimony of the early Roman law itself, which looks upon this as a peace-offering. At the same time there is evidence in ancient law of the parties paying for the decision of the dispute. The two talents paid by the disputants in the Homeric legend find their counterpart in the Hindu law which provides that the

1. Muirhead, *Roman Law*, p. 182, Sohm, *Institutes of Roman Law*, p. 231 note.

party losing has to pay to the king an amount equivalent to the amount decreed, to pay for the trouble taken by him or his judge. But whatever that may be, the great importance attached to the oath and the religious part of the litigation indicates that the chief operative element in the suppression of the private feud was not so much the authority of the King or the Elders as the sanction of religion.

CHAPTER VIII

LAWS OF CRIMES AND CRIMINAL PROCEDURE

ABSENCE OF CRIMINAL LAW PROPER IN ANCIENT LAWS : While violent wrongs were undoubtedly the first to be remedied by Civil law, a notable feature of many ancient codes of law is that the element of genuine Criminal law is entirely absent from them. The *Leges Barbarorum* are more or less tariffs of damages payable for particular wrongs, pre-eminently violent wrongs, such as murder and maiming. The *wehrgeld* or composition payable for every offence is fixed. In the *Njals Saga* we find how coolly murders committed by members the family or slaves are compounded for between heads of the families. The Anglo-Saxon Codes are also tariffs of damages. Early Roman law too provides only civil remedies for wrongs and there is no regular procedure by which crimes may be *punished* instead of being compounded for.

When an offence roused the resentment of the entire community it would be punished in early Rome as an act of State, by the Legislature itself.

MAINE ON THE EVOLUTION OF CRIMINAL LAW : In course of time, as Maine points out, cases of this character are referred in Rome to special committees or *Quæstores* of the legislature. As the occasions for the appointment of *Quæstores* multiply, permanent *Quæstores* are appointed who would deal with particular classes of cases. These *Quæstores* are thus gradually transformed into regular courts for the decision of criminal cases of a particular character.

The action of the state for the punishment of offences was called forth originally, by acts directed against the state alone, or possibly by an outrageous offence which roused the wrath of the entire community. Gradually however the state begins to take a larger view of its functions and interests and undertakes the punishment of other offences. This process goes on till a whole class of criminal offences is established. These offences are distinguished from *delict* in this that they are punished by the state either by corporal punishment or by fines, while a *delict* is compensated by payment of damages to the wronged party, though the amount of the damage itself may be penal rather than reparatory. It seems also that the Romans gradually developed the theory, that crimes were violations of the right of the state. But, even then, the state did not rise to the sense of its rights in the matter of private wrongs like theft or assault all at once ; but gradually extended its activities towards punishing these as people began to develop a wider notion of its rights.

This, in brief, is the history of Criminal law in Rome according to Maine. But this is not the whole story even in respect of the law of Rome nor a history that we find followed everywhere. It would be altogether unjustifiable to conclude from this that the concept of offence was necessarily later in legal history than that of *delict*.

CRIME AND REVENGE : To get a real grasp of the significance of ancient law in Rome or Germany we have to take the laws and social institutions all together. When we consider the laws as supplemented by other social institutions, we shall find that, while the laws speak of compensation for wrongs, there are beside the laws other ways in which offences are dealt with. In the *Njals Saga*, while the heads of families are coolly compounding for the deaths of their slaves and dependants, other members of the family are planning revenge, and revenge they do have and are justified in having. That represents primitive society before the administration of criminal justice was known. When a person was injured he would have his revenge, and his society, his kinsmen would aid him in having his revenge.

As we have seen before, the state's first act of interference with this self-redress took the shape of arbitration, for the purpose, primarily of determining the extent to which vengeance was justified and, later, for awarding an equivalent as damages for the injury. This was originally only an alternative remedy for the injury. The wronged party might agree to have his revenge bought off. That is as far as the law would go. If the compensation was deemed inadequate, there was always the right of seeking revenge. Compulsory composition came later, and when it did come, it was often got round by secret murders as we find in the *Njals Saga* and also in the vendettas of much later days.

There was also another factor by the side of the reparatory law which helped to keep society in order. There was religion with its code of sins and punishments after death, to be compounded for by penances and expiations in this world. The religious organisation of society was more ancient than the state and its sanctions were, in those days, much more effective than mere human sanctions. Everywhere, in primitive and ancient times, we find penances imposed by religious law for offences long before crimes are punished by the state. The punishments imposed by religion were sometimes very drastic. Death, maiming, disfigurement and a wild variety of physical chatisements were included in the schedule of penances. On the other hand there were drastic social sanctions, extending from more or less harmless privations to the utter exclusions of a member from society, as in the case of the *Homo sacer* or *ærarius* of Rome or the *abhisasta* of India. So that, before the state undertook to punish offences, the idea of offence and punishment had already become familiar to the people in the religious law.

There is a remarkable circumstance to be noticed in the scheme of sins and their appropriate penances. Penances are provided as less drastic substitutes of punishment in after life. We therefore find lurid pictures of the punishment people suffer after death for sins committed during life. Maine has drawn attention to the fact that these punishments in hell are conceived very largely on the principle of retaliation, the infliction of approximately the same injury on the wrong-doer that he has inflicted on his victim.[1] Generally speaking the retaliation of justice in hell takes the shape of a much severer injury than the sinner has caused in life. At other places, the punishment draws its appropriateness from some injury being inflicted on the offending limb or some other fanciful punishment the clue to whose psychological basis we have probably lost. It is probable that these pictures of hell are merely aggravated

1. Maine, *Early Law and Custom*, Chap. II.

forms of what actually prevailed in the society of those days. The penances prescribed for the sins also partake of the same character more or less. Penances for injuries caused to others very often take the shape of the voluntary infliction of the identical injury on the wrong-doer himself. Occasionally we notice the idea of reparation. At other times the offending limb is punished. In this way the early law of penance seeks to approximate, in its punishments, to the injury which the wronged party would like to inflict on the wrong-doer. In the developed Indian Law of penance, there is moreover the idea of purification of the mind by self-mortification, worship or contemplation, most notably associated with sins not affecting others. But there is enough material in this law of penances to justify the conclusion that religious society in primitive times sought to check offences by punishing them through penances and, in inflicting these punishments they were largely influenced by the standards of the law of self-redress.

¶It is in this religious code of Sin and Penance, which existed side by side with the reparatory code of civil law in primitive society that we have to seek the roots of a law of Crimes. Even in Rome, it seems probable that the legislature was moved to inflict punishments on parricides and similar offenders very largely by reason of the fact that the offence was very seriously against religion. In India we find that at quite an early age the king comes in to assist the religious law and inflict punishments on offenders against religion and incidentally punishes some violent wrongs. It seems probable that in India punishment of violent offences came into existence before civil actions. It was the same in Persia. The *Vendidad* speaks in terms of corporal punishments of wrongs, though later interpretation of the law has transformed the *Aspahe Astra* and the *Sraosha Charana* into formulæ for expressing the measure of damages.

The king intervened to compel people to perform appropriate penances for their offences and he made his might felt by inflicting punishments himself. He also intervened to regulate self-redress. He took the vengeance out of the wronged party by inflicting a punishment on the wrong-doer which would satisfy the injured party. This interposition in the matter of self-help and of penances evidently laid the foundation of the criminal jurisdiction of the king.

The interposition of the king depended very largely on the position which he held in society. The chief of a clan who is only *primus inter pares* is not likely to be able to assume the authority to punish a clansman. That seems to have been the position of the chiefs in Cæsar's Germany. There was therefore no criminal jurisdiction of the chief though civil arbitration prevailed and very likely private revenge and blood-feud prospered except in times of war, when the magistrates or tribal chief had the power of life and death for preventing offences.[1] In India on the contrary, the community settled down in peace very early and the king stood out as a very superior person with boundless power and very great sanctity. It is here therefore that we find criminal jurisprudence grow much quicker than elsewhere. In ancient Rome the king was never very much above his people and what pre-eminence the king had was extinguished by the early establishment of the republic. The authority of the state therefore in punishing crimes was slow in growing up there.

In India therefore we find a wholesome criminal jurisprudence is established much earlier than elsewhere. Originating in private revenge and the concept of punishment in religious law it quickly developed a theory of the obligation of the king to protect his people by the punishment of criminals. At a very early epoch, the criminal law here has entirely shed its association with the *lex talionis* and we find private revenge rigorously put down and reduced to a perfectly modern rule of private defence. Corporal punishments, including death, maiming, whipping and other very severe penalties, as well as imprisonment and fine are inflicted, at first by a fixed tariff, but gradually in accordance with a rule of justice in which due consideration is given to the circumstances of the case, the age

1. Cæsar quoted by Vinogradoff, *op. cit*, Vol. I, p. 345. It is noticeable that Cæsar distinguishes between the magistrates who "*vitæ nescisque habeant potestatem*" and the *principes regionum* who '*jus dicunt controversiasque minuunt*" implying the administration of civil justice by arbitration and not criminal justice by punishment.

and position of parties, the moral and educational standard of the offender and every other circumstance which is relevant to Criminal justice.[1]

In course of time Hindu law develops a philosophy of Criminal justice which reveals the root of the criminal jurisdiction of the king in the religious law of penance. *Dharma* is the eternal order of things and regulates the whole world as well as the life of men. When a man commits a sin he violates *Dharma*. To adjust the equilibrium of *Dharma*, it appears in this world as *danda* or punishment[2]. When a sinner gets his punishment from the king his sin is wiped out just as much as it would be by penance. The king is bound to give appropriate *danda* to the offender, though there is a slight recognition of his right of pardon[3] in later law. If he fails to inflict the appropriate punishment through weakness or error, the offender is relieved of his sin, but the offence falls on the king and he must perform an appropriate penance to satisfy the outraged *Dharma*.[4]. Nay more, if the king fails to keep his people on the right path by inflicting appropriate punishments, all the sin that they do by reason of the want of protection falls on the king.[5]

It is thus seen that the king or the state acquires an interest in the punishment of offences by reason of its association with religion. The state is protected by *Dharma* and if *Dharma* is not maintained the state falls to pieces. This indicates the historical origin of the interest of the state in the punishment of crimes. India never passed beyond this stage of dependence of law on religion. But in other places when law ceased to be associated with religion, the interest of the state in the punishment of crimes continued for other reasons and other philosophical justification had to be sought for the punishment of crimes.

---

1. Yajnavalkya. I. 368.
"The king should inflict punishment on those deserving it after knowing (considering) the nature of the offence, the place, the time, the strength (of the offender), his age, occuption and wealth," also Manu VII, 16, *Apastamba* XII, 51.
2. Manu, VII, 14. 18, 22-28. Yajnavalkya, I., 354.
3. *Apastamba*, XII, 52.
4. Gautama, XII, 48.
5. Yajnavalkya, I, 337.

CHAPTER IX

CIVIL ACTIONS AND EVIDENCE

A.—Law of Evidence

NO RULE OF PROCEDURE OR EVIDENCE IN PRIMITIVE LAW : From what has been said before it will be clear that primitive judicial procedure was chiefly concerned with the determination of the amount of justified revenge or reparation. A proper law of procedure or evidence is no part of this action. The community through its accredited heads interposes in a dispute simply for the purpose of seeing fair play.

Gradually, however, the need for rules of procedure begins to be felt. The earliest part of these rules are rules of evidence, or principles for the determination of questions of fact when facts are in dispute. It need not be assumed that the earliest interposition of the community or the state in a dispute must have involved a determination of questions of fact. On the contrary, it is quite conceivable that the state interposed only for the determination of the amount of justified revenge or composition where the fact of the injury was not in question. Questions of fact seem to have rarely troubled people in ancient times where people lived in small communities in which everyone knew about everybody else's affairs very well. In the *Njals Saga* the murders which are compounded for by the heads of families never seem to have raised troublesome questions of fact. The facts were taken for granted. The only question to determine was the amount of compensation. Soon, however, disputes would arise in which facts were not undisputed ; one side averred facts which the other side disputed. The community would have to decide in such cases what the facts were.

DIVINE TESTIMONY THE MEANS FOR DECIDING ON FACTS : How was this to be done ? The normal course in modern society would be to take evidence on both sides and weigh their respective values. That is the procedure which we find developed at a very early stage in Hindu law, where the earliest extant laws lay down that the king was to determine the truth from the testimony of witnesses. So too in other early systems in which judicial procedure has become fairly developed. But by a critical examination even of these sources we can trace the existence of an earlier stage which existed everywhere. In all ancient systems of law there is, by the side of the testimony of witnesses, another means of deciding on facts, namely, ordeal or appeal to divine testimony. Besides, the testimony of witnesses also was really tested by divine sanctions. The evidence considered was evidence given on oath. When a man takes an oath, he is invoking the gods to bear witness to the truth of his assertions and, the idea is that he is laying himself open to certain divine judgment if he speaks an untruth on oath. This indicates that in its origin even the testimony of witnesses depended for their value on supernatural testimony. This is indicated by the Hindu law, in which oath is regarded as a species of divine testimony (*divya*). The belief is also clearly expressed that if a man takes a false oath he always suffers punishment by miraculous means.

This leads us back to an earlier stage of legal procedure in which the only means for the determination of the truth about facts in dispute was an appeal to the gods in some form or other. We must remember that in most cases the judges were the entire community, of which the accused was a member and generally speaking, the facts of the case would be known to them personally. No question of proving facts therefore would ordinarily arise. Where the facts were known to none of these persons, what other means could these rude people have, but to call upon the gods to show what was the truth ? Generally speaking, however, it seems that divine testimony was appealed to when the judges were *prima facie* convinced of the guilt of the accused person. Where judges decide upon their personal knowledge this would very often be the case, for no one would be lightly charged with an offence where the fact was not more or less notorious. In each case the accused could appeal to divine testimony against the human knowledge.

ORDEAL : There have been various forms of ordeal in different parts of the ancient world and amongst backward races of to-day.[1] Ancient Indian law and usage had various modes which ultimately survived in four chief forms recognised in judicial procedure—the ordeal by fire, by water, by the balance and by poison. The fire or water or other instrument of divine testimony is first sanctified with magic formulæ by which it becomes changed with divine power so that through its action the judgment of the gods is indicated. We may see that as society progresses, ordeals tend to grow more and more humanised. The absolutely primitive ordeals are such that no man could come harmless through them except by a miracle or by accident or fraud ; and the test would normally terminate in death, in the absence of a miracle. But ordeals in more developed societies are neither so very impossible nor so drastic in their consequences. Thus, while the fire test in absolutely primitive society generally requires one not to get burnt after entering a blazing fire, the same test in later Hindu texts involves only the placing of a red-hot iron-ball on the palms of one's hands which is fairly well-covered with leaves, crushed grains and grass. With this red-hot ball the accused goes round a marked spot for seven times. If his hands are not burnt he is not guilty. This test might be successfully gone through, and, if it failed, it did not kill the accused but only burnt his hands.

JUDICIAL COMBAT : The judicial combat was a special form of appeal to divine testimony which we seldom find in the most primitive strata of law. There is a great deal to be aid in favour of the view that it is really a survival of the primitive private vengeance with a modified significance. An injury led to conflicts between opposing groups and a single combat between leaders of opposing groups was often resorted to as a substitute for a general fight. Of this single combat we find numerous instances not only in the *Mahabharata* but also in definite historical instances in ancient India. It was also a common institution among Norsemen. Both in India and amongst the Teutonic races we find the association in course of time of the issue of this single combat with the intervention of the gods. In India the view that in such fights the gods

1. For various forms of ordeal see Hastings' *Encyclopedia of Religion and Ethics* under *Ordeal*.

sided with the right, does not seem to have led to the development of this single combat as a means for determining the rights between parties in a litigation. This however was what happened among the Germans ; and, in the Middle Ages, this became one of the most usual modes of determining disputes as between knights. In England judicial combat by hired champions flourished very long.

OATHS : The mildest form of appeal to divine testimony is the oath. It is founded on the generally received belief that when a person makes a statement with a definite formula or with a particular formality, the gods would miraculously punish him if he speaks an untruth. The earliest idea seems to have been to let a man clear himself by his own oath. This seems indicated by some texts of Hindu law. But a more familiar institution is the compurgation, an institution of the Middle Ages, which had its roots in remoter past. In this procedure a number of persons, belonging to the group to which the accused belonged, came forward to swear to the innocence of the accused person. They were not witnesses ; their chief value seems to have originally consisted in adding strength to the divine testimony implied in the oath of the accused.

OATH ORIGINALLY A FORM OF DIVINE PROOF : The value of the oath at this stage, whether it is the oath of the defendant or that of his compurgators, lies in the appeal to divine testimony. When a man takes an oath, he lays himself open to punishment by miracle. If he is not punished, that is divine proof of the truth of his assertion. It is on this basis that the defendant was apparently let off. But a stage is soon reached at which the complainant also offers, and is permitted to offer his oath, and possibly the oath of his kinsmen against that of the accused. In such cases it was probable that an ordeal would be the normal resort.

WEIGHING OF EVIDENCE GRADUALLY DEVELOPED : But eventually, out of this placing of oath against oath is evolved the practice of judging between opposing oaths or the weighing of testimony of witnesses. Some such history of the origin of a law of evidence may perhaps be indicated by the provisions of some ancient systems of law insisting upon a minimum number of witnesses in favour of a party. The number was probably the original number of compurgators. The fact that witnesses have to take their oaths and thus place themselves under the judgment of gods is also suggestive of the ultimate historical origin of the law of evidence in the ordeal and appeal to divine testimony.

SLOW DEVELOPMENT OF A RATIONAL LAW OF EVIDENCE : A historical study of the ancient Indian law of evidence shows how tardily the essential idea in the modern law of evidence, that the evidence has to be weighed by reference to experience about probabilities in order to ascertain the truth, grew up in ancient society. The earliest rules of evidence are hemmed in by artificial rules with regard to the number of necessary witnesses, the classes of persons whose evidence can be received, the variations in the law of evidence with reference to the witness's castes and so on. As we go on, we find these artificial rules dropping off, till, in the latest of the *smriti* texts the most common-sense rules for testing and weighing evidence are laid down.

EVIDENCE TENDS TO PUSH BACK DIVINE TESTIMONY : When the evidence of witnesses as means for deciding on facts is evolved it does not mean that divine testimony is altogether abolished. On the contrary, all ancient systems of law have ordeals by the side of a law of evidence. Even compurgation survives, as it did in the wager of law in England, long after courts have begun to weigh facts. But the testimony of witnesses tends to push the other forms of proof more and more to the background. In the Hindu Law of the later *smritis* for instance, ordeal is not permitted where human testimony exists. In some other text it is retained as the last resource of persons who are accused of very grave offences for clearing themselves. In all other cases *divya* is disallowed. In this way divine testimony gradually disappears before human testimony, as society advances and the judicial tribunals get greater experience in weighing evidence.

GROWTH OF DOCUMENTARY EVIDENCE : It is hardly necessary for me to mention that the human testimony is always the oral evidence of witnesses in ancient systems of law. Documents come into existence much later and they are at first given very scanty recognition. In Babylon and in Egypt where the early spread of the art of writing led people to embody their judicial acts in fixed and unalterable form of documents, the evidentiary value of documents naturally became very high. In early Hindu law, although writings was at that time known, written evidence (*lekhya*) is never mentioned as a form of proof. When we find it first mentioned as a mode of proof, documentary evidence has not yet acquired anything like the importance of the sworn testimony of witnesses. In the later code of Yajnavalkya, on the contrary, the testimony of documents is considered to be of greater weight than the testimony of witnesses. This corresponds to the growth of a spreading habit of embodying legal transactions in documents, testified to by other texts of Yajnavalkya.

RELIGIOUS ELEMENT IN THE LAW OF PROCEDURE : The fact that divine testimony was the sole means for determining the truth about matters in dispute naturally made litigation an essentially religious institution. I have referred before to this feature of ancient judicial procedure. The *Legis actio Sacramento* in Rome, and litigation generally, was so far a religious institution that the Pontiffs entirely controlled it. They determined the *dies fasti* and the *dies nefasti* and declared the auspices which must be observed in litigation. They *formulæ* essential for a litigation were only known to them. In fact, no litigation could be commenced or carried on without the assistance of the Pontiffs. The religious character of litigation is even more pronounced in Hindu law. It is not only because the law administered is a part of religion and is known to and interpreted by sacred caste that litigation is looked upon as sacred. Another and perhaps a more important reason is that in litigation the important thing is to determine the truth—which could only be done by appeal to divine tests by way of ordeals or oaths. In each case special formula of magic import had to be uttered to bring down the power of the gods for the determination of truth.

FORMALISM OF ANCIENT PROCEDURE : The association of litigation with religion accounts for much of the formalism which is a pronounced feature of the ancient judicial procedure. Formalism is almost always intimately associated with magic. When a transaction is supposed to lead to supernatural consequences, primitive mind naturally tends to attach the supernatural consequence to some definite thing said or done in the transaction. This word or act of magic import is therefore repeated with scrupulous accuracy by every one who wishes to produce the same consequences. In this way there grows up the formalism of rituals. Natural reasons may explain the first prototype of the ritual, but magic alone explains, in most cases, why the ritual is followed in all cases. Litigation, in so far as it always called gods to witness, was a very important ritual, every step of which was instinct with magic and must therefore be scrupulously followed. A single false step, an unsuspected lapse in going through the formality might spoil its magic effect and make the appeal to divine testimony entirely futile. That is why primitive and ancient trials are so formal and elaborate. And this original formalism, when it has become habitual, sticks to litigation and law long after they have shed their religious associations, as they did in Rome.

B.—Initiatory and Execution Proceedings

PRIMITIVE COURTS ONLY DECIDED DISPUTES : There is one important feature of ancient juridical procedure which must not be forgotten. I have mentioned before, that ancient adjudication only sought to regulate self-help. The right of every person to seek revenge or reparation of an injury by his own efforts and those of his kinsmen was recognised. The king or the arbitrator or the community only sought to determine the extent of the reparation he would be entitled to claim. Or, in other words, the early courts only decided disputes. A modern judicial procedure involves not merely the decision of disputes, but also, in the first instance, the summoning of the defendant and witnesses and, after the decision is given, the execution of the decree. In early judicial procedure, on the other hand, these things are entirely left to self-help. In the *Legis Actio* procedure, the *in jus vocatio* was entirely an act of the party. It was the plaintiff's business to take the defendant to the court and, for this purpose, he had a right of arrest (*manus injectio*) in some circumstances. In Germanic laws we find the summons given by the party in a set form.[1] In India, in the earliest laws we hear nothing of any process of the king to summon the defendant or the witnesses. Though in the developed judicial procedure it is laid down that the court must summon the defendant and the witnesses by its own officers, it appears that in the earlier stages, the plaintiff had the right to prevent the defendant, by fear of supernatural punishment it may be, from evading justice and even arresting him for the purpose of taking him to court.

EXECUTION OF JUDGMENT IN ANCIENT LAWS : In the matter of execution of judgment also the position seems to have been similar. When a judgment had been delivered—and it must be remembered that all these ancient judgments, where they were not for a measure of revenge, were for payments of certain sums of money—it became a debt and the judgment creditor could only realise that debt by his own power. The two familiar ways of enforcing repayment of debt were arrest of person and distraint of the goods of the debtor. This was not the right of the judgment creditor only. but of all creditors. We read in Hindu law that a creditor was entitled by law to realise his debt by means of force or fraud, restraint or various other forms of constraint.[2] And if a debtor complained against that, all the king could do was to compel him to pay the debt.[3] In Rome we find a *nexal* creditor was entitled to arrest the person (*manus injectio*) or distrain all his goods (*pignoris capio*). Maine has pointed out the existence of this custom of distress amongst the Irish, Germanic and other races also. In India there are also other modes of realising debts of which fasting at the door of another was one of the most characteristic.[4] This meant bringing down injury by supernatural agency on the householder and as a means of restraint, it was hardly less effective than arrest or attachment of goods.

1. Vinogradoff, *op. cit.*, I, 353.
2. Manu, VIII, 50.
2. Yajnavalkya, II, 40.
4. *Acharita* in Manu, VIII, 50.

GROWTH OF JUDICIAL PROCESSES FOR SUMMONS AND EXECUTION: The judgment creditor was thrown on his own resources therefore, for enforcing his decree though his rights were of a very drastic character. The enforcement of these rights depended upon his own power to do so. Besides, the enforcement of rights in this way led to trouble. We therefore find that in course of time every society develops a procedure in which judges undertake not merely to decide disputes when they are brought before them, but also to bring the necessary parties, and their witnesses before them by the use of the State authority and when a decree is passed, to compel the judgment debtor to obey it by means of processes of execution. The history of this evolution has been different in different countries and the forms which the laws have taken have widely varied; but the tendency of the laws to provide processes of this character is universal.

I have mentioned before that the early judicial remedies were always in the form of decree for the payment of a certain sum of money. The formula of the Roman Law always stated in the *condemnatio* that the judex was to condemn the defendant in a sum of money stated in the formula or a sum to be determined by the judex *ex æquo et bono*. The Germanic laws are all in the character of tariffs for the payment of sums of money for different varieties of injury which may be inflicted. We see the same thing to a certain extent in the very early Indian law. In England, law *i.e.*, the common law, could only give remedies in the form of damages in a certain sum of money, except in a limited number of real actions and it was only by the intervention of equity that other modes of enforcing judgments which would be more adequate was made possible. This arose from the fact that primitive judicial procedure was in the form of a composition for justified revenge, the plaintiff being compelled to receive money-damages in lieu of retaliation.

Sooner or later however, every system of judicial procedure discovers that money damages do not give ample remedies in all cases of wrong and gradually develops processes for giving specific restitution of property or enjoining a party from doing a wrong and such other remedies. The development of the resources of adjudication while it shows itself in the multiplication of wrongs for which remedies are provided, is also manifested in the provision of new forms of remedy for those wrongs.

C.—Topics of Law

EVOLUTION OF LAW AS INDICATED BY TOPICS OF LAW: Some light may be obtained with regard to the question of the evolution of law generally from a study of the primitive judicial processes. If we look into the primitive laws of the Semites or of the various Germanic races we find that the great bulk of their laws consists of penalties for personal violences. In the *Legis Actio Sacramento* we find a much more advanced condition of society in which two persons are found disputing their rights to some property. But the point to note is this that the Prætor does not interfere until the parties are threatening violence to one another. In Hindu law also we find, the same early origin of law, in the repeated insistence in early law on the king's duty to prevent violence and theft. There is abundant evidence in Hindu Law to show that the first things that the king sought to prevent by means of judicial remedies were *sâhasas* and it was only gradually that other forms of wrongs came under the cognisance of law. A *sâhasa* originally meant something done with violence. It came however to include many things later on and to be at one stage identical with crimes generally. But the rudimentary idea is that of a violent wrong. It seems to be fairly evident that in primitive society the interference of the community either in the clan or in the more developed society, tribe or state was due to a violence done or threatened. And legal remedies originated in such interference.

The earliest form of injury relating to property which we find redressed is probably theft. In some societies adultery as well as theft are punished to the same extent as personal violence. A close study of the topics of litigation in India shows that, quite early in the history of laws, debt is a head of litigation side by side with the violence, offences and theft. We see the same thing in the laws of other countries. The first distinctively civil action which is recognised in law is, generally speaking, an action for the recovery of a debt. What could have led to this circumstance can only be imagined. Some clue to this inclusion of debt side by side with theft and violent offences may be found in a consideration of the nature of debt in ancient law. Everywhere we find that the penalties provided for non-payment of debt are of a very drastic character. In Rome the debtor, if he failed to pay, could be made the bondsman of the creditor or sold as a slave or even be cut into pieces and shared by his creditors in revenge. In Hindu law the creditor is fully entitled to have recourse to any kind of force or fraud for the purpose of enforcing payment and the debtor has no remedy against such self-help on the part of the creditor. The Hindu law also gives an insight into the psychology of the earliest days in the conception of the terrible condition of a debtor in hell if he died without payment of his debt. All these indicate that non-payment of debt was looked upon as a species of crime. It was, in a way, on the same footing as theft inasmuch as, like theft, it was appropriating what was not one's own. This seems to have been the reason why we find debts amongst the earliest topics of litigation in ancient times in India as elsewhere. Next to debt, an action for the recovery of property wrongfully taken by another, even where there is no violence, comes into prominence. These three classes of actions, namely, actions for violence to one's person, for non-payment of debts and for recovery of things wrongfully taken, lie at the root of the entire evolution of the various forms of civil law. The course which the history has actually followed in different countries have varied greatly but I think it can be laid down as a general proposition that these three forms of action were the roots out of which the entire civil law was gradually evolved.

CHAPTER X

THE LAW OF PROPERTY

PROPRIETARY RIGHTS: Property is perhaps the most important and the most complicated and extensive branch of modern laws. In proprietary rights we distinguish various kinds of rights, ranging from mere occupation or detention of a thing to ownership. When a man is in physical contact with, or has actual control over, any property he is said to have the detention of it. When this detention is accompanied by a right to possession which could be enforced against any person who sought to interfere with the right, it is called the right of possession. But ownership is a much fuller right which implies not merely the right of possession but in fact an absolute power to deal with the property as one chooses, subject, no doubt, to the rights of other people and of the state. Between these limits lie a large range of proprietary rights of a more or less limited character.

THEORIES OF THE ORIGIN OF PROPERTY: Jurists have often speculated about the origin of property. Blackstone thought that the right of ownership belonged, by the law of nature, to the first occupant, or in other words that ownership arose out of occupation. Savigny, speaking of the Roman law only, says that, according to that law, property originates in adverse possession, ripened by prescription, or, in other words, that when a person has been for a sufficiently long time in possession of a thing he is deemed to be the owner of it. This is not identical with Blackstone's theory but is a statement of a historical fact and has nothing to do with the origin of ownership as a human institution. But this has been made the foundation of a theory that property originates in occupation.

MAINE'S THEORY: Maine combats this proposition and points out that, in the first place, it is not the first possession which constitutes the essential part of property in early Roman law, or anywhere else, but rather the element of long continuance which is represented by the Roman concept of prescription. It is not therefore proper to say that ownership originates in occupancy. It would, according to him, be truer to say that the doctrine of occupancy follows at a latter date, when the right of ownership is already well-established and every thing is regarded as necessarily importing the existence of an owner. In the second place, Maine points out that this theory, as well as all theories of a similar character, supposes that man owned property in primitive society as an individual. But, in point of fact, it was not the individual but the corporation of which the individual was a member that really mattered in primitive society.

Maine's thesis, based upon his reading of the village communities of India, of Russia and of the Slavonic races of the Balkans is that in the most ancient times property belonged jointly to the entire village, which consisted of people who actually were or supposed themselves to be descended from a common ancestor. These villages were thus similar to the Roman *gentes* or German Hauses. In course of time property came to be temporarily divided between different families and we find this system in the Russian villages. Still later, the property is divided permanently so that the shares assigned become the absolute property of the families, as in the Indian village community.

Defects in Maine's Theory : One of the chief foundations of Maine's theory has been seriously disturbed by the further study of the Indian village communities, which shows that the type of the village communities which Maine describes is not the only type, nor perhaps the most primitive type of the village in India. Baden Powell, with a command over far ampler material than was available to Maine, established beyond doubt that the *ryotwari* village in which the lands were the absolute seperate properties of the families was apparently the more primitive form of village community. The lands really were the seperate property of the villagers although some common functions were performed by the village officials. According to Baden Powell, the communal village, in which the lands were jointly held and apportioned between the families for enjoyment, was a development out of the original *ryotwari* type of villages in which the land was held by each family separately. The existence of village communities in ancient Anglo-Saxon society, upon which a great deal of reliance was placed by Seebohm, has been severely criticised by Pollock and Maitland who have pointed out that these communal institutions were not primitive and that individual ownership existed, in point of fact, at least as far back as you can carry communal ownership.

There is reason also for holding that joint ownership of property by the family was not necessarily the most primitive form of ownership. On the contrary, looking at the most primitive strata of Indian law one is disposed to conclude that the right of the individual in the shape of the father was recognised in the beginning and it was only by a gradual process of limitation of the father's rights that the joint ownership of the father and sons was established. In the primitive law in India as elsewhere, so far from the son being looked upon as co-owner of property, he himself was, as we have seen before, looked upon more or less as the absolute property of the father. It was probably when society was scandalised by the unnatural conduct of a father in exercising his authority over the son against the dictates of natural affection and religious duty that limitations were placed upon the father's rights such as we find in the provision of the *Twelve Tables*,[1] that when a father sells his son thrice into slavery he is deprived of the right of fatherhood ; or the provision repeated in the early Hindu law that the father should not alienate the family property so as to deprive his son altogether of maintenance. In course of time these restrictions were developed in ancient India into what is supposed to be the chracteristic of Hindu law, though it was not really universal or primitive in Hindu society, namely, the *Mitakshara* conception of joint ownership of the father and sons.

---

1. A somewhat similar idea is sound in Sunahsepa's answer to his father who had sold him to be sacrificed but claimed him back when he was saved. Sunahsepa did not answer that by sale the father had lost his right, but urged that the father had lost his right by reason of his cruelty in agreeing to kill the son, conduct so heinous that it is not even found among Sudras. *Aitareya Brahmana* (translation in Maxmuller's H.A.S.L. Panini office Ed., p. 215).

IMPORTANT FACTS OF THE HISTORY—MOVABLES RECOGNISED AS PROPERTY LONG BEFORE LAND : With respect to the other branch of Maine's proposition, namely, that property did not originate in occupation, it is no doubt out of question to formulate an exact history of the early origin of property in the graphic style of Blackstone or to proceed upon the assumption that primitive men started on the basis of mutual convenience to establish rules which are most conformable to the sense of fitness of things of the modern man. This is no doubt not justifiable nor is it possible perhaps, as a matter of jurisprudence, to lay down how the notion of property actually originated. But it is worth while noticing a few facts of early legal history and of societies in a primitive state of civilisation, which perhaps give a clue to its genesis and early history. The first of these facts is that immovable property was recognised by men at a much later date than movable property. People had their ownership established in movables like cattle, sheep or household goods or slaves long before land became the subject of ownership. When property in land came to be recognised the notion of property was already there and all that was necessary was simply to include land among the various kinds of properties. This we find illustrated by a large mass of evidence, of which I shall mention to you only the fact that even in early Roman law, land was not recognised as *Res Mancipi*. It is possible that at that time land had not much value. Whatever use land might be put to was made by all people in common. But at a later date when land became valuable, and it was looked upon as property, all that the Romans had to do was to classify this property with the *Res Mancipi* and thereby attract to it all the provision of the law relating to property of that description.

POSSESSION ALONE PROTECTED IN EARLY LAW : The next point to note is that apparently the earliest remedies in respect of properties were remedies for recovering possession or damages in respect of things which are in a person's possession. This is most prominently illustrated in the Germanic laws where the right of pursuit belongs to the person who is not necessarily the owner, but the possessor of the property.

Similarly, later on, legal remedies were also available, primarily in respect of possession. Pollock and Maitland have very clearly brought out the fact that all the actions available under early English law for recovering real property, were essentially possessory actions. In point of fact, property really represents little more than old possession in English law, till the law is modified by recent statutes.[1]

PROPERTY PROBABLY DEVELOPED OUT OF POSSESSION : What do these things indicate ? Do they not make it very possible, firstly, that in the infancy of society it was actual possession of things which people habitually respected ? It is impossible to say how this respect for possession could have arisen.[2] We may imagine that when the society awoke to self-consciousness in respect to this fact they found that a person in possession of a thing which was regarded as being of any significance was, as a matter of fact, allowed to retain such possession ; and as the tendency of primitive men is primarily to follow custom, this continued to be the law. When this was the law, the only kinds of property or things in respect of which any proprietary rights could be conceived, were movables. At a later date, permanent possession and right to possession became dissociated from the mere fact of temporary actual possession and the rudiments of property may have thus been established as involving a right to enjoyment or right to exercise power over things. When agriculture developed and waste lands were brought very largely under cultivation, this notion of ownership became gradually transferred to land.

PROPERTY DID NOT NECESSARILY INVOLVE ABSOLUTE POWER OF DISPOSITION : Another important fact to note about the

1. Pollock and Maitland, *History of English Law*, Vol. II. Ch. IV.

2. Fustel de Coulanges in *The Ancient City* puts forward a theory *re* the religious origin of property growing round the sacred fire. The theory, besides being highly conjectural, labours under the serious defect that it practically seeks to identify property with land. If, as is clear, considerable advance was made in the notion of property before land came to be recognised as property, it is hardly necessary to build up the notion of property round the house-fire. The growth of agriculture and pressure upon land would easily explain the growth of the conception of property in land without lobouring the religious theory.

primitive and ancient notion of property is that it did not imply, as the concept of property implies to-day, absolute and complete control over the subject-matter of property. Ownership implied a right of enjoyment and, in so far as enjoyment implied a destruction by consumption of the property, it implied a right to destroy. But alienation of property was very seldom contemplated ; at any rate, in respect of immovable property it does not seem to have been contemplated at all in early times. So soon, however, as people began to acquire the habit of alienating immovable property, we find restrictions growing up in various forms in various societies ; and underlying all these restrictions we find the growing notion that immovable property is the fund for the maintenance of the family. In Hindu law, as I have said elsewhere, these restrictions ultimately matured into a notion of joint ownership of father and sons in ancestral immovable properties.

We get it then that, to start with, the notion of property developed round movables long before agriculture was known and land became valuable. The notion of property at this stage could not have been materially different from the notion of possession. In fact, even at a much later stage of evolution of the concepts, property and possession were not really differentiated, though different grades of possession were distinguished. When land became useful it gradually came to be recognised as property.

Joint ownership of land in early law : It is here that we come up against the notion of joint ownership. Joint ownership in some form or other is found to exist in the early stages of many societies. Thus for instance in ancient Germany land was annually redistributed between the families of the village, and each family became owner of the produce of the land allotted to it. In Greece on the contrary land was allotted to families permanently, but the harvest was brought to a common granary and enjoyed in common. Besides these there are the various types of village communities referred to by Maine, in India, Russia and the Highlands of Scotland. In Rome too it is probable that at one time the *Ager Romanus* was public property and was let out for cultivation on payment of a *vectigal* or rent.

Even where lands are distributed among the families, we find, in many cases, that limitations of various degrees are placed on the powers of the head of the family in respect of its enjoyment. Restraints of various grades are imposed upon the alienation of the landed property in the interest of heirs, till we find such restraints maturing into the recognition of a right of co-ownership of sons and grandsons.

From these facts it has been concluded, that land was at one time common to the entire village and it was by gradual stages allotted to families absolutely. Even when it was so allotted, it continued to be the joint property of the family and it gradually became individual property. The evidence at our disposal hardly justifies this elaborate conclusion. On the contrary, such restrictions as we find can easily be explained on an absolutely non-communistic basis.

FORMS OF LAND TENURE EVOLVED UNDER THE PRESSURE OF ECONOMIC ENVIRONMENTS : Let us conceive a community just settling down to agriculture. So long as they were nomads they had no need for land. The whole world was their land. But when they settled down as agriculturists, land acquired greater importance for them. So long, however, as there was plenty of land available, every one squatted where he liked and cultivated what land he could. We must remember that primitive cultivation did not necessarily imply ownership of land. Even at this day, Kukis carry on cultivation on the *jhum* system over entire hillsides in Tippera and Assam and shift from place to place every year. It was only when agriculture became fairly developed and systematic and the population sufficiently large, that questions of possession of land for purposes of cultivation became of importance. It now became important that every family should have enough to cultivate and none should have an unfair advantage. All the various forms of restrictions of property rights in land may have normally arisen out of this need for the adjustment of the agricultural needs of the entier community. Under different cultural and economic environments the various differing systems may have arisen quite independently. Some of these forms may have evolved out of others, but there are no materials on the basis of which we can say that any specific form was the evolute of any other. Far less is there any reason to justify our placing all the forms of land organisation in one chain of progressive evolution. The Highland system may have been the most primitive as Maine supposes, or, as is more likely, it may have been the result of a long course of evolution out of any of the other systems under the influence of the special environments in which the Highland clans were placed.

THERE IS NO COMMUNISM IN EARLY ARYAN LAW : It seems certain however that the Aryan race, before their separation, did not have communal agriculture or communal ownership. The remotest antiquities of India, Rome, and Greece alike negative the idea and in India itself communal and joint family ownership were almost demonstrably later institutions developed under the influence of their special environments, after land had become an asset of value more or less limited in supply. With regard to the restraints on the alienation of property it is almost demonstrable that they were not parts of the primitive law. Thus in Indian law we find on the one hand kings in the Vedic times performing the *Visvajit* sacrifice at which they gave away everything they had without regard to the interests of their sons. We find Haris Chandra giving away his kingdom to Viswamitra and selling away his wife and son and himself into slavery. All this is conceived as possible. On the contrary we find a text of the law stating that "land is given only with the consent of one's village, one's kinsmen, the chief and of one's heirs (*dayada*)." We have limitations likewise on the powers of a person in the alienation of immovable property, because "those who are born, those unborn and those who are in the mother's womb, all look forward (to it) for their maintenance."

GROWTH OF RESTRAINTS ON ALIENATIONS : These conflicting laws can be understood if we remember what we observed in an earlier chapter, *viz.*, that early legal statements are very often too wide or too narrow. As time goes on limitations have to be placed on them in order to make them correspond with the actual law. It would appear that in the earliest stage of ownership it is stated to be absolute, without necessarily implying a really free disposition of property, for the simple reason that alienation was very exceptional—the man who had got a property usually kept it. In course of time as alienations came to be desired and law-givers found that the freedom was being exercised beyond the limits which could have been contemplated in the original law, restrictions began to be imposed. When land belonged to a family, the head was of course the owner, without any restraints on his powers to start with. But when owners actually sought to alienate land so as to deprive the family of its maintenance out of the land, which was either not really contemplated in early times, or which was contrary to expectations formed by long usage, the right of the owner was sought to be more narrowly interpreted. The owner was supposed to be incapable of alienating land without the consent of his sons and grandsons ; or, in other places, he was prevented from alienating the entire property or the bulk of the property so as to leave the family without adequate maintenance. In India, as I have said before, these limitations grow and develop till a school of jurists of a later age interpret them as implying a right of sons by birth in ancestral immovables. Elsewhere it ended in the provision of an inalienable fraction of the property *cr legitim*.

Similarly when land in a village was owned by a villager, it was understood that he would occupy it himself. If he did alienate it, he would naturally give or sell it to his co-villagers. In course of time however there may have arisen the possibility of a sale out of the village. But when the lawyers said that this was not permissible without the consent of the villagers, they were not necessarily stating a new fact, but they were making a new law in so far as they were applying in some form the tacit presupposition of the old law to new facts.

It is out of question, as has been observed before, to try to frame a general course of evolution which must have been followed by the law of property everywhere. In historical times we know that not only different courses have been followed in different societies, but the courses have sometimes been totally contradictory to one another. In some societies we find that restrictions on alienation are emphasised and made more rigorous, till landed property gets altogether fixed in families. In other societies, which started with identical institutions, the restrictions such as they were, are gradually explained away and eliminated till the power of free disposition is reached. One thing is quite clear, however, that restrictions on the enjoyment or alienation of property was no part of the earliest laws of man in an society whatsoever. Property (which, as we have seen, is indistinguishable from possession in primitive law) when it is first conceived, is supposed to involve unqualified powers. Restrictions on those powers are imposed later. On the other hand, disposition of any property as a fact was an exception rather than the rule in primitive society.

RESTRICTIONS ON ALIENATION IN ENGLISH LAW : At a fairly early stage of social history everywhere we find restrictions are imposed on the power of free alienation, either in the interest of the heirs or of that of the entire community. Some restrictions are also imposed in the interest of the royal revenue, where, as in India, land furnished a substantial revenue to the State. The result of this is a fairly complex system of rules which lend themselves to various lines of development under varying influences. At some stages of evolution we find a tendency to discourage alienation. At others, society tends to encourage free circulation. A fine historical illustration of the way in which the opposing forces sometimes alternate in the history of the same society is furnished by English law. The history of English Real Property Law after the conquest opens with inalienable estates. The tenant in fee, whether simple or in tail, holds a life-interest and his heirs take a vested interest after him. We find however that in course of time the courts begin to explain away the words vesting estates in heirs as words of limitation and not words of purchase. The legislature at one time sets its face against the freedom of alienation in respect of estates tail at least, but in course of time lawyers again contrive to find fictitious processes by which to defeat these provisions of the legislature. The result of the conflict of the opposing forces encouraging and discouraging alienation has been the ultimate freeing of landed property from all restraints.

IN INDIAN LAW : In India we find the opposing tendencies working through the entire course of history and giving rise to conflicting texts relating to the disposition of property. Conflicting tendencies are noticed in later history of law as well. Commentators and text-writers working on the basis of this conflicting body of laws arrive at contrary conclusions, so that, ultimately, while Vijnaneswara declares the father and sons equal owners of property, Jimutavahana on the contrary stands out for the absolute ownership in law, of the father, subject to moral restraints which do not invalidate alienation by the father, if made without totally depriving the heirs.

DETERMINING FACTORS IN THE HISTORY OF RESTRAINTS ON ALIENATION : These two opposite tendencies are found to operate alternately or together in the history of every progressive race. Alienation is sought to be restrained in the interest of heirs and co-villagers. On the contrary there are sound social reasons why alienation should be sought to be promoted. As trade and commerce increases, there must grow up a feeling in favour of free circulation of property. That is perhaps why in Babylon of all the ancient states, we find the greatest freedom in the matter of alienation of all kinds of property. But commerce was not the only force which operated in favour of alienations of property. A very potent factor in this respect has been religion. Religious gifts form a part of the earliest laws and institutions of India. Gifts most favoured in the earliest days of India were gifts of cows, and later, of gold and, apparently still later, of land. And as time went on, we find the great religious merit of gifts to Brahmans extolled. At a much later date, in the controversies about the alienability of land we find the strongest arguments centring round gifts for religious purposes. In England too, the influence of the Church went a great way towards removing the shackles on alienation of land. Gifts to Churches and religious bodies must have become very common, enough to cause alarm, before the Statutes of Mortmain were passed. Yet again, it was in the interest very largely of the religious houses that the Mortmain Acts were circumvented by the Use. By the time the Statute of Uses was passed, the Use had acquired a considerable standing and other great interests had centred round it, but the interests of the Church still played an important part in the circumvention of the Statute of Uses and the creation of the modern Trust.

CLASSIFICATION OF PROPERTY : As soon as we find a law of property, along with restrictions on the alienation of property we find, in every system of law, a classification of property. Starting with the theory that property was originally incapable of free alienation, Maine looks upon this classification as one of the devices by means of which the first steps towards free alienation were taken. As we have seen, there are good reasons for demurring to Maine's thesis about the antiquity of restraints on alienation. Maine's statement is undoubtedly true to this extent however that restraints on alienation invariably go with a classification of property. In no primitive law do we find restraints in respect of all kinds of property. There are some which are deemed to be of greater value than others and it is these which are hemmed in by restrictions. In fact the classification of properties in primitive and ancient law gives us a very important clue to the relative value attached to the various species of property at the time when the classification first came into existence. In Roman law we find the distinction between *Res Mancipi* and *Res nec Mancipi* at the very start of the historical epoch. *Res Mancipi* originally included implements of agriculture, slaves and cattle, but not land. This indicates that while agriculture had risen to considerable importance, land was not yet property. So soon as land becomes property, it is included under *Res Mancipi*.

It was probably some such reason of importance that lay at the root of the distinctions between various classes of property everywhere. One class of property is superior to another, whether by reason of its economic or social or religious value. Some classes of property give a higher social status, irrespective of their economic value. Or again some kind of property may be of superior religious interest. The hearth and home, for instance, was intimately associated with the religious life of the ancients and, on that account, prized above every other kind of property. For one reason or another, one class of property was placed in a position of superiority over another and thus gradually classifications of property were evolved.

It was a historical accident perhaps that Hindu jurists stumbled upon the scientific distinction of movable and immovable property from the very earliest stages of the law.

Immovable property (*sthavara*) was placed in a category apart. To it was assimilated the slave and, later on, certain incorporal rights called *Nibandhas* in the *Dharmasastras*. But in the beginning immovable property was distinguished as a category apart. It is hardly likely that we should ever be able to know precisely the reason which lay behind this superiority of land. It was assuredly not the earliest kind of property known. There was apparently a time when cattle were the most valued kind of property. The distinction given to land at a later date may have been due to purely economic reasons, such as, for instance, the superior stability of this kind of property, or it may have been due to religious reasons, such as are suggested by Fustel de Coulanges, in so far as landed property grew up round the sacred hearth, or simply to the fact of the enormous importance which agriculture acquired in the society.

CHAPTER XI

LAW OF CONTRACT

CONTRACT IN MODERN LAW : If you take up a modern code or Encyclopedia of the laws you will find a general principle, subject to some limitations, natural or artificial, that where a man has promised to do or abstain from doing a thing under circumstances under which the promisee would actually act on the faith of it, he is bound to keep that promise. In different systems of law different conditions are necessary so that the promise may become actionable. In English and British Indian law, what is required is that the promise must be accompanied by a consideration, unless it is embodied in an instrument executed with certain formalities. It is different in France and Germany. But the differences are only different efforts of the legal mind under diverse conditions to find the true limitation to the general principle which would make the doctrine workable and equitable.

The doctrine is really of wider application than this. The promise made and accepted is only a species of agreement, which is essentially a union of two wills. Where two minds are at one that something shall be done or abstained from, it shall be done or abstained from, if the agreement satisfies the other conditions of validity. That is how you may state the modern law of contract.

It is a very comprehensive concept and embraces a very wide range of legal rights and obligations. In a sense a sale or absolute transfer of ownership is a contract in so far as it is a juristic act founded on consent. But where, as in a sale, the effect of an act founded on consent is in substance to terminate the jural relations between the parties, it is convenient to exclude the transaction from the sphere of contract and limit the term to cases where outstanding rights and obligations are created by the transaction. There are many cases of transfer of property however which create contractual obligations, such as lease, mortgage, etc. Marriage in modern law is a species of contract. Debt, deposit, contract of marriage and numerous other transactions are looked upon as only species of contracts.

ABSENCE OF A GENERAL CONCEPT OF CONTRACT IN ANCIENT LAW : If you look at ancient systems of law, even fairly developed ones, you will find this concept conspicuous by its absence. You will find debt, lease, sale, agreement of service, pledge, exchange, agreement to sell, promise to give and so on, but no general conception of contract. Take, for instance Hindu law as you find it in the advanced codes of Narada or Brihaspati. You find several heads of obligations which modern jurisprudence would bring together under the common concept of contract. There are debt, deposit, pledge, promise of gift, partnership, contract of service for wages, leases and other contracts relating to land, and sale. But Hindu law knows nothing of a general theory of contract, under which all these various transactions might be brought. In Babylon we have a very highly developed commercial law and contractual relations from a large part of the laws of the country. But there too there is no general theory of contract. Even in Roman law which has given us the word, it is doubtful how far a general theory of contract was developed before the days of the glossators, that is, before Roman law ceased to be the territorial law of Rome.

MAINE ON THE HISTORY OF THE LAW OF CONTRACT : The fact is, that a general theory of contract has everywhere been the result of a generalisation made by jurists from a number of legal relations which were evolved without reference to any such theory. The earliest notable attempt to trace a history of the evolution with reference to Roman law was made by M ine. His theory is that all contracts are ultimately derived from sales. The earliest form of contracts in Rome was the *Nexum*.

The original *Nexum* according to Maine was a sale on credit. Mancipation was a sale for cash. When however the price was not paid, the parties remained bound to each other to complete the ceremony by payment of the price. That is how the notion of obligation originated. Later on *Nexum* developed into a transaction by which loans were given and debts created. It was an extremely formal transaction with copper and the scales and its legal effects depended entirely on the proper performance of the entire ceremony, the actuality of the consent of the parties being hardly material.

The special importance of the *Nexum* lay in the power it gave to the creditor over the debtor, the power to make the debtor his bondsman if he failed to pay the debt. When this power was abolished, *Nexum* gradually went out of use and its formalities were dropped. The essential thing in the transaction was now supposed to be the transfer of property from the creditor to the debtor. This idea led to the development of new forms of contract in which the formalities of the *Nexum* were absent but this essential feature, the transfer of ownership was retained. Thus grew the Real Contracts, *Mutuum, Commodatum, Depositum and Pignus*, in all of which the obligation of the debtor arises from the fact that property has been transferred to him by the creditor.

Later on, according to Maine, even this form was dropped and it was found possible to create obligations only by a form of words. This is how, according to him the *Stipulatio* was developed. The Literal contract was also similarly developed by the substitution of a form of writing for a form of speech. The special form hit upon was, according to Maine, the result of the careful book-keeping habits of Romans.

This process of gradual dropping off of unessential elements culminated, according to Maine, in the evolution of the consensual contract in which no formality was necessary, nor anything except mutual consent. In these, the essential character of contract is found to disentangle itself from the non-essential forms which encumber its earlier stages. There were only four kinds of such contracts : sale, letting and hiring, partnership and agency, which could be created by mere agreement. At a later date, reliefs were given in other cases of mere agreement unaccompanied by any form or transfer of property. These were the *pacta adjecta* of civil law, the *pactum de non patendo* of Prætorian law and pacts to pay *dos* by Imperial law. That is as far as Roman law ever went.

MAINE'S THEORY CORRECT IN OUTLINE : The bare outline of Maine's theory is undoubtedly sound, though its details are not satisfactory. The notion of contract as such was unknown in very ancient times. Such contracts as were known were recognised not on account of the element of consent but on account of some other accidental, formal element. The element of agreement in such transactions as the essential thing in them got disentangled from other factors in the course of history and a general theory of contract was thus established. These are the undoubted truths in Maine's theory.

THE EVOLUTION OF CONTRACT IN ROME : So far as the history of Roman Law is concerned, the evolution of the contract of *Mutuum* by the dropping off of the formalities of *Nexum* is also indubitably accurate. This cannot be said of his theory about the other forms of Real contracts. And Maine is undoubtedly wrong in deriving the Verbal and Literal contracts from Real contracts, by a dropping of formalities.

VERBAL CONTRACT : The older form of verbal contract in Rome was the *sponsio* which was a part of the religious law and belonged to the earliest stratum of the law. The *Stipulation* is clearly derived from this religious promise by the substitution of other verbs for the magic verb *spondere*. Instead of saying "*spondesne ? spondeo*" the parties say in this form, "*Promittis ? promitto,*" "*Dabis ? dabo,*" etc. It seems probable that the *Stipulatio* was originally designed for the *peregrin* to whom the *sponsio* was forbidden. In any case the derivation of the verbal contract from the *sponsio* of religious law is quite clear. It has no connection with the Real contract or the *Nexum*.

LITERAL CONTRACT : The Literal contract too had a history of its own entirely independent of the Real contract. The Romans were very careful accountants and entries in their account books with regard to a loan were, naturally enough, looked upon as good evidence of a debt. There can be no doubt that account books first got admitted into the law as evidence. It is conceivable that, in order to make the evidence quite convincing and free from doubt a practice may have developed of insisting on a special form of entry—the *codex transscripticium*—made in the presence of the debtor. When an entry of this character in an account book was proved, it may have grown usual to look upon the entry as conclusive evidence. From this it is but one step for the entry in an account book to rise to the rank of a special form of contract, instead of being merely evidence of a contract. When contracts were hemmed in by so many subtleties of form and proof of contracts was often so difficult, creditors would naturally avail themselves of an opportunity of having their contracts embodied in a *codex transscripticium*, to avoid troubles of formality and proof.

CONSENSUAL CONTRACT—SALE : The Consensual contracts on the other hand were obviously derived from other sources. *Emtio Venditio* is clearly an evolution out of Mancipation through the intermediate stage of sale by tradition. When the formalities of sale dropped off, and payment of cash price became immaterial for the legal validity of a transfer, it was but one further step to dispense with the immediate delivery of property as well. The result would be that just as the cash price of the purchaser was replaced by an obligation to pay the price, so the delivery of possession by the vendor is replaced by an obligation to deliver possession. The unilateral obligation thus leads on to the bilateral.

PARTNERSHIP : Partnership also is indirectly derived from sale. The history of other systems of law, such as the Babylonian, shows, what Roman laws do not clearly indicate, that partnership originated in joint purchase of property. In Hindu law we notice, as perhaps the earliest form of partnership, the association of several priests in the performance of the complicated sacrifices ; but that also leads us back to an ulterior source in joint acquisition of ownership. When things are acquired jointly the relations of the joint purchasers can only be stated in terms of obligations. The joint ownership of things leads on to a joint ownership of business, a concept which is familiar to the joint family law of India. The law of partnership is only a more developed form of the law for determining the relations of co-owners with reference to a business.

AGENCY : *Mandatum* apparently had an entirely independent source. The idea of representation of the head of a family by another member seems to have been a familiar feature of ancient society. A man might act through his son or his slave and have the benefit of or be responsible for the acts of the son or the slave. Gradually the usage is developed, entrusting the commission to an independent party instead of the son or the slave. The relations between such agent and the principal would follow the analogy of the relations between the head of the family and the member who represents him. When consensual contracts were developed, this form of relationship naturally fell under the category, and the general principles of contractual obligations modified the incidents of the rights.

The history of Roman law does not therefore bear out the conclusions of Maine except in bare outline. Besides Maine has confined his attention too exclusively to the purely legal history. But law proper in ancient times represented only a fraction of the whole law. A great part of the effective laws belonged to religious systems. Thus though Maine is quite correct in saying that a contract as such was not enforced in primitive and ancient *jus* it would not be correct to say that the ideas of the obligatoriness of a promise as such was unknown in very ancient times.

CONTRACTS IN RELIGIOUS LAW—VOWS TO GODS : The obligatoriness of contracts as such in religious law enforced by supernatural sanctions is indicated by the very ancient stories of contracts with gods. A very ancient Indian story on the subject is the story of Sunahsepha. There we hear of king Harishchandra having made a vow to the god Varuna that if the god gave him a son he would sacrifice the son to Varuna. We hear later on, how Harishchandra put off the god from day to day and ultimately the son, who had grown up, refused to be sacrificed, and left for the woods. The result was an illness of Harishchandra which promised to be fatal. Here we have all the elements of a pure contract. There is no formality. It is a mental promise to the god and becomes binding so soon as the god does his part of the bargain. And, further on, we find that there can be a satisfaction for the contract by substituting something else for the thing promised as was done in this case.

This is a good illustration, but in fact, contracts of this character with gods go back to far remoter antiquity. The notion that promises made to the gods must be kept, at any rate, if the gods have given the *quid pro quo*, belongs practically to the infancy of humanity. The vows to the gods are merely applications of known human relations to superhuman beings. It follows therefore that in societies which insisted upon the sanctity of vows made to the gods the sanctity and the obligatoriness of promises in religious law was already known. In fact we find that, at the earliest stages of the evolution of law almost everywhere, promises made in the presence of gods or in the name of the gods were regarded as binding in religion, and in some cases such sacred promises are also enforced in law.

OTHER SACRED VOWS : In Rome, among promises which were thus enforceable by virtue of their sanctity we find the marriage vows and the *sponsio*. There were, no doubt certain formalities associated with these vows, forms, which were regarded as essential in order to bring the promise within the cognisance of the gods, but there is little doubt that the essential thing—the thing that was enforced, was the promise as such. Another notable promise of this kind was the sacred wager, of which we find one illustration, and only an illustration, in the wager laid in the *Legis Actio Sacramento*. When a man asserts a state of things and makes a solemn promise to lose a certain sum if his assertion proves false, he becomes thereby a debtor to the gods ; and if his statement proves false, he must fulfil his promise. That is why the *sacramentum* was such a decisive factor in the little drama of litigation of ancient Rome. All these are forms of promises by reason of which the promisor is bound to the gods.

HAND-GRASP : Another illustration of a similar sacred promise is furnished by the hand-grasp which is common to the Germans and Romans. Here the hand is mutually offered and grasped as a pledge to the gods for the performance of his promise.

FESTUCA : Another form of promise amongst the Germans was the one which was solemnised by the delivery of a *festuca*, or a little rod, which appears under different forms in different Germanic races. In these forms of religious promise, the element of promise is overladen with a certain amount of formality. But there can be no doubt that as a matter of religion, the obligatoriness of solemn promise, at any rate in some forms, was recognised at an early stage of law.

PROMISES IN LAW : The recognition of the bare promise in *Law* was a much later institution. Many things are found to have been known, many relations amongst men well-established, long before they are recognised as a subject for judicial determination. The fact that people knew of the sanctity of promises did not necessarily imply that the courts would take cognisance of it. The jurisdiction of courts in early law is found to have been strictly limited to certain topic. Contract became a topic of law and an appropriate action was found for it comparatively late in the history of judical procedure.

EVOLUTION OF DEBT : The earliest civil action known to law appears to have been an action to recover a thing which has been wrongfully taken away. The *Legis Actio Sacramento* of Rome is strictly speaking appropriate to this action only. Even in English law, the earliest actions seem to have been real actions for the recovery of things. The earliest form of contract known to law proper appears to have been debt. It appears very early in all ancient systems of law. So soon as society settles down to agriculture and business, credit becomes a necessity, barter and sale will be made on credit. So we find debts realised by the State by the most drastic penalties. The condition of the *nexal debtor* in Rome was very severe because the law was supremely anxious to secure repayment of debts. The debtor in ancient India was in an equally desperate position. The creditor had absolute freedom in the realisation of his debt and could avail himself of all forms of force, fraud and coercion to get back his money. Over and above this, there were the terrors of punishment in Hell for the debtor who has died with his debt unrequited.

We have seen that Maine derives the *Nexum* from the *Mancipation* and considers the original *Nexum* to have been merely a sale on credit. Pollock and Maitland have arrived at the same conclusion with reference to Germanic laws. There can be no doubt that sale on credit was one of the origins of debt. But it seems probable that debts arising out of other transactions were known from an equally early date. In the antiquities of Hindu law debts are found to arise out of a *promise* to pay in the earliest extant records. Besides there is no reason why we should not derive the obligation of debt from the loan for use as from sale and barter. In the earliest days of society, men would borrow each other's cattle or agricultural implements for temporary use. The taking of a thing for use would make a debt as well as an incomplete sale.

There is one circumstance which seems to indicate the priority of the loan for use. Debts appear to have originally become actionable on the analogy of Real actions. We have no definite history of the derivation of the forms of action in Roman law, but it is now possible to have a clear history of the evolution of the various actions in English Law. This discloses the interesting fact that a debt became originally actionable on the analogy of Real action. The *præcipe in capite* was the action for the recovery of land. In Glanvill, the original writ of debt is a close copy of the *præcipe in capite*. Pollock and Maitland point out that the original idea in debt was that of *recovering what was one's own*, no idea of a personal obligation ever entered into it.[1]. One would expect this idea to develop more naturally out of a *Commodatum* than of a sale on credit. It is as probable therefore that debt should have been derived from a loan for use as from a sale on credit and I am disposed to think that both these sources contributed to the birth of the concept of debt.

In course of time we find the notion of a personal obligation replacing the proprietary idea in debt, and debts founded on causes not originally recognised in law are assimilated with the law. The debt of promise founded on the religious law takes its place by the debt arising from the taking of a thing. The *sponsio* becomes recognised in civil courts.

PLEDGE—SURETYSHIP : This leads to the development of other forms of contract. Two of the earliest known forms of

1 Pollock and Maitland, *History of English Law*, Voll. II, p. 204.

contract after debt were contracts of suretyship and pledge. In Hindu law and Roman law we find this contract in a highly developed form, as a species of personal obligation arising out of a promise or delivery of goods. It is possible to trace back the history of these forms of contracts to a much earlier stage by a study of Germanic customs. The original form of pledge and suretyship in Germanic Law was the *borh* who was originally a hostage—a kinsman given away as a slave of the creditor, to be redeemed by the debtor by the payment of the money due. This existed long before debt proper was known, for securities had to be given for the *bot* or the blood-money which might be due from one. An alternative and later form of pledge was the *wed*, which consisted of a property of equal or greater value than the amount of the debt, which was given to the creditor absolutely, the debtor being understood to have the right to recover the thing on payment of the money due.[1].

Out of these rudimentary institutions the contracts of suretyship and pledge are gradually developed, when credit is well-established and the faith of people more relied on. The word of an honest and substantial man comes gradually to be considered as good as having him as a hostage. A similar development made it possible to dispense with the transfer of ownership in the thing pledged. The *Mancipatio fiducia* is replaced by the *Pignus* and, still later, at a much more advanced stage of society a *Hypothec* is considered a perfectly good security.

DEBT AND PLEDGE IN RELIGIOUS LAW—GAMBLING AND WAGERING : The concept of debt and security are developed very early in most ancient societies and we find reflections of it in the religious law, sometimes in very fantastic forms, at a very early stage of the evolution of law. I have already spoken of the wager of which we find an illustration in the *sacramentum* of the *Legis Actio Sacramento*. Wagering was only one form of pledge. The thing wagered was the security for the fulfilment of the promise and was forfeited if the promisor failed to make good his representation. This, we find, was developed into an advanced code of gambling, at any rate

1 Kohler, *The Pledge Ideal*—in Kocourek and Wigmore, *op. cit.*

among most of the Aryan races. Gambling with dice was a very ancient institution in India. Kingdoms were pawned away, wives and children and, lastly, the players themselves were given away as slaves. And when people lost their wagers they accepted the situation. Tacitus, describing the Germans, gives a description which might apply word for word to the ancient India. "What is marvellous," he says "playing at dice is one of their most serious employments ; and even sober, they are gamesters : nay, so desperately do they venture upon the chance of winning or losing that when their whole substance is played away, they stake their liberty and their persons upon one last throw. The loser goes calmly into voluntary bondage. However younger he be, however stronger, he tamely suffers himself to be bound and sold by the winner."

The notion of debt represented to the ancients the highest degree of obligation conceivable. This is indicated by the fact that in the earliest days of ancient India, the obligations which a man owed to his ancestors, to the gods and to the *rishis* are described as the three debts with which a man is born. By having a son one redeems a debt to ancestors. Remarkably similar is the idea of the German described by Tacitus. The young Sattans when they arrive at maturity let their hair and beards continue to grow until they have killed an enemy. When they have killed an enemy they shave and "they allege that they have now acquitted themselves of the debt and duty contracted by their birth." It is probable that the hair and beard was considered as a pledge for the satisfaction of the debt.

Diverse sources of the law of obligation : It is not necessary to trace the history of every form of contract from its earliest roots. From what I have observed, however, it would be clear that the course of evolution of contract is not a simple one of uniform development from a single original. Sale and barter have undoubtedly been two of the chief sources out of which the notion of contract was evolved. But this was not the only root of contract. An equally important source was the religious duty of keeping faith, which gradually comes within the purview of law proper and largely moulds and affects it.

In the course of its further history the domain of contract has been enriched by contributions from other allied institutions. The institution of hostages helps to develop a law of pledge, that of representation by members of family leads to the institution of agency ; slavery makes its contribution to the law of free service ; religion is contributing its quota all along the line. The result is a very complicated and diversified history which has naturally not been identical everywhere in the world. In the course of this history we find a large number of legal relations growing up, which are found by systematic students of the law at a later age to be essentially founded on consensus of parties, though in legal theory the obligatoriness is often held to attach to some other accidental circumstance. Gradually the element of consensus asserts itself as the essential element of the transactions and they are all brought under one common head of transactions founded on mutual consent or *Contract*. This final evolution is the result of legal science, the effect of the scientific study of jural relations. But the consummation was not achieved by the unaided efforts of science. In many places we find historical accidents have greatly contributed to the result.

HISTORY OF CONTRACT IN ENGLISH LAW—SCIENCE AND HISTORY : The history of the English law of contract may be referred to as a fine illustration of the course of evolution of the notion of contract out of consensual transactions which were, in the beginning, looked upon as owing their obligatoriness to other circumstances than consensus. This does not mean that this history gives us anything like a general course of evolution which we may expect to find followed in other places. The English history only gives a fine illustration of the action of science and history, logic and accident, in a more or less haphazard fashion on the evolution of law.

English law was founded on Germanic law. From that source it got a formal contract, only the particular formality of the seal was derived from Roman law. This sealed promise, enforced by the Action of Covenant forms the earliest contract enforced by the courts. The other contractual actions were those of Debt, Detinue and Account, but the gist of these actions was not conceived to lie in agreement, but the delivery of property and, in the Action of Account, in the existence of a certain relationship. I have said before how debt and detinue were evolved out of the Real action, *præcipe in capite*.

The true contract in English law, other than the covenant, became actionable much later, when *assumpsit* was evolved. But *assumpsit* was a trespass on the case and, in its origin it was an action of damages for malfeasance, where, by reason of the wrong-doer having come upon the thing by permission, trespass would not lie. In course of time however *assumpsit* grew more and more contractual till the element of assumption or the promise formed the gist of the action.

This was a historical accident. English law already knew of contract ; and a promise, without more, was already actionable, if it was given a certain form. There is no logical reason why in the course of evolution, the formalities should not have dropped off this agreement and the simple contract evolved out of the Action of Covenant. Besides, there were the actions of Debt and Detinue, essentially contractual, which might, by natural evolution, have led to the general concept of a contract. But, as most frequently happens, this obvious and rational development did not take place and the element of agreement in the Covenant, Debt or Detinue was not disentangled from its accidental associations till the concept of simple contract was evolved by a historical accident out of an action for a tort.

When *assumpsit* had become an action proper to the enforcement of a simple promise, there remained beside it other contractual relations which were even then not assimilated to the agreement. Debt and Detinue continued to have an independent existence. And they might have remained distinct, but for the fact that owing to the rule of wager of law, Debt and Detinue were very inconvenient remedies. Attempts were gradually made therefore to bring cases of Debt and Detinue under *Assumpsit* by a sort of legal jugglery. When this effort succeeded it had an important consequence for jurisprudence. As the chief contractual transactions were brought together under the form of *Assumpsit*, the common elements underlying them naturally became prominent and this led at last to the evolution of a general law of contract.

CHAPTER XII

The Law of Descent—I

In most settled societies of primitive and ancient times we find that after the death of a person his property is inherited in accordance with some settled rule of law. In some ancient societies we find a certain measure of liberty given to the individual to regulate the devolution of property after death. But testamentary succession seems to be the exception rather than the rule in ancient societies. Maine concludes from this that a law of intestate succession always precedes any rule of testamentary succession.

Origin of the law of intestate succession : Attempts have been made by jurists to trace the law of intestate succession to more primary elements. A theory which was familiar to classical Roman jurists, and has persisted down to modern times, refers the law of inheritance to family ownership which is supposed to have been the most primitive condition of things. When the property belonged to the family, the death of the head of the family made very little difference. The headship passed to another member of the family, but the property remained, as before, family property. When individual ownership came to be recognised, what was the order of succession to the headship under the older law now became an order of inheritance.

Family ownership and Law of inheritance : We have already seen that the evidence available does not warrant the conclusion that ownership was originally joint. The probabilities are rather in favour of individual ownership leading on to collective ownership by gradual restriction of the owner's rights. Similarly, it may be said that it is more likely that the law of inheritance may have led to family ownership rather than *vice versa*. "We have but to ask for a time, when testamentary dispositions are unknown and land is rarely sold or given away. In such a time, a law of intestate succession will take deep root in men's thoughts and habits. The son will know that if he lives long enough, he will succeed his father ; the father will know that in the ordinary course of events his land will pass from him to his sons. What else should happen to it ? He does not want to sell, for there is none to buy ; and whither could he go and what could he do if he sold his land ? Perhaps the very idea of a sale of land has not been conceived. In course of time, as wealth is amassed, there are purchasers for land ; also there are bishops and priests desirous of acquiring land by gift and willing to offer spiritual benefits in return. Then the struggle begins, and law must decide whether the claims of expectant heirs can be defeated. In the past those claims have been protected, not so much by law as by economic conditions...... But now there must be law. The form that the law takes will be determined by the relative strength of the conflicting forces. It will be a compromise, a series of compromises and we have no warrant for the belief that there will be a steady movement in one direction, or that the claims of heirs must always be growing feebler.... Other and different arrangements were made elsewhere, some more, some less favourable to the heirs, and we must not assume without proof that those which are most favourable to the heirs are in the normal order of events the most primitive. They imply, as already said, that a son can hale his father in a court of law and demand a partition ; when this can be done there is no 'patriarchalism,' there is little paternal power."[1]

FUSTEL DE COULANGES ON THE ORIGIN OF LAW OF INHERITANCE : Fustel de Coulanges derives the entire law of inheritance from the religious beliefs of ancient times. The right of property according to him was established for the accomplishment of hereditary worship. It follows that it was not possible that this right should fail after the short life of an individual. The man dies, the worship remains ; the fire must not be extinguished. So long as domestic religion continued the right of property had to continue with it.

"Two things are closely allied in the creeds as well as in the laws of the ancients—the family worship and its property.

1 Pollock and Maitland, *History of English Law*, Vol. II, p. 249 *seq.*

It was therefore a rule without exception, in both Greek and Roman law that a property could not be acquired without the worship, worship without the property.... It was same in India.

"From this principle were derived all the rules regulating the right of succession among the ancients. The first is that the domestic religion being, as we have seen, hereditary from male to male, property is the same. As the son is the natural continuator of the religion, he also inherits the estate. Thus the rule of inheritance is found ;.... The father need not make a will ; the son inherits of full right.....

"To form an idea of inheritance among the ancients, we must not figure to ourselves a fortune which passes from the hands of one to those of another. The fortune is immovable, like the hearth, and the tomb to which it is attached. It is the man, who, as the family unrolls its generations, arrives at his hour appointed to continue the worship, and to take care of the domain."[1]

CRITICISM OF THE THEORY : In discussing Fustell de Coulanges's theory of the origin of property I pointed out that he makes the fatal blunder of identifying property with land. On the contrary, even in Rome and Greece, to which he confines his observations, movable property preceded immovable property and as a matter of fact the law of property was fairly developed with reference to movables before property in land was recognised. Here also he considers the law of inheritance exclusively in connection with land. But a law of inheritance apparently existed before land became property and weapons and cattle, women and possibly slaves passed to heirs. Besides, the entire theory hinges upon a theory of primitive family ownership, which there are good reasons for doubting.

It cannot be denied of course that in ancient societies, notably in Greece, Rome and in India, property has been associated with religious rites and there is an intimate association of the heir with the performance of obsequial rites and the offering of periodic repasts to the deceased and his ancestors. But the Indian evidence leaves little doubt that the

1 Fustel de Coulanges, *The Ancient City.*

supposed dependence of inheritance on the offering of oblations to the deceased is a comparatively late growth. The heir was usually the person who offered the funeral repasts, but the heirship does not appear to have been dependent on the *pinda*. The earliest statements of the law in the *dharma sutras* are not only singularly free from all reference to offering of oblations but the order of succession too does not exactly correspond to the order of persons entitled to offer *pindas*. The entire theory with regard to the dependence of the Hindu law of succession on the spiritual benefit conferred by the heir is based on texts of Manu and ignore altogether the historically anterior law. But even in Manu there is no dependence but rather a mere co-existence of the two functions of heirship and giving of oblations. The co-existence must be quite patent in the most usual cases of succession and from such observed co-existences a later theory sought to deduce the right of inheritance from the spiritual benefit conferred. But even in later law this proposition was not free from dispute and it was only in the *Dayabhaga* of Jimutavahana among extant works that we find a consistent attempt to work out the theory of spiritual benefit.

Similarly, we find that in Rome the *Twelve Tables* makes no reference to the doctrine of spiritual benefit. But the heir was as a rule bound to offer funeral repasts and from that, a later theory in Cicero's time drew the conclusion that succession depended on the offering of funeral repasts. The evidence that we have, therefore, does not justify the conclusion that the principle underlying inheritance in primitive law was the provision for funeral repasts for the dead. The doctrine appears to have been a later deduction.

These theories therefore do not enable us to go behind the law of intestate succession. As far back as law takes us, either in primitive law or in the customs of backward races, a law of inheritance already exists. But a guess may be hazarded as to the probable origin of a rule of intestate succession.

EARLY RECORDS OF DISTRIBUTION OF PROPERTY BEFORE DEATH : In the *Vedas* we hear of a father dividing his property amongst his sons in his life-time. A somewhat later, though sufficiently early, evidence shows us the husband dividing his properties between his two wives before renouncing the world at the appointed age. This seems to have been the primary state of affairs before any rules of inheritance became settled. In India, men were expected to renounce the world and spend their days in religious contemplation in the woods, when they attained old age. Before so retiring, they could dispose of their properties as they chose. Although not exactly in this form, we find that in other societies also old men had to renounce the world or die. It is probable that they were permitted to distribute their wealth before they left. At a time when there was no settled rule of inheritance, this was apparently the only mode in which devolution of property could be settled.

The element of caprice in such distribution must have been at a minimum. Men in primitive times habitually followed precedent. When a leading man of the society is found to have acted in one way, others simply imitate ; and in this way customary schemes of distribution of property seem to have been evolved by repetition and to have led on to a law of inheritance.

TESTAMENTARY AND INTESTATE SUCCESSION : If this view is correct it would run counter to the favourite theory, started probably for the first time by Maine that in primitive society the will of the owner had no share in the devolution of property and that testamentary succession followed intestate succession. This view is, in part, based on the theory of joint ownership of the family and the community which we have found reason to doubt. In so far as this theory asserts that regular testaments came into existence later than the law of intestate succession, there can be no doubt of its truth. But if the suggestion I have ventured to make above is correct, the root of intestate succession itself will have to be sought in some form of rudimentary testament. It would then appear that owners of property disposed of their goods in their lifetime. In course of time this crystallised into a law of intestate succession. Once a rule of law is established it tends to restrain the freedom of disposition of the proprietor. We should therefore expect to find laws seeking to restrain dispositions of property against the law of inheritance. Such rules we can find in Rome, in Greece and in India. But in spite of this, some power of disposition, more or less limited, was always retained in the proprietor. This appears in Hindu law in the freedom of the father to distinguish between sons in the distribution of his property. The early law is more or less unsettled as to the exact limitations on the father's power, but we notice that in course of time the limitations close more and more upon this freedom. In Rome this power develops into a right of testation by a declaration in the *Comitia Calata*. Amongst Germanic races Tacitus found no power of testation, but Anglo-Saxons developed testamentary dispositions of land quite early and rudiments of testamentary powers are traceable among other Germanic races. No doubt all this was very different from the testament as it developed in the later history of Rome, but the two things have sprung from the same root.

ORDER OF INTESTATE SUCCESSION : The order of intestate succession in any society depends entirely on the principles of social organisation and kinship. As a general principle it may be laid down that every rule seeks to give the inheritance to the person who is presumably nearest and in most intimate touch with the deceased. This statement however would be correct only within limits ; for social organisation changes sooner than the law, and it is a very usual thing to find the law very imperfectly representing the feelings of people as regards nearness of kindred, by reason of the fact that the law belongs to a stage of social organisation which is past.

It is not possible to lay down any hard and fast general rule as to what constitutes nearness of kindred according to the feelings of the people. Even a son is not always the best loved and the nearest kinsman. On the contrary, amongst matricentric families, most notably in those that are polyandrous, a man's son is more or less a stranger to him, while his sister's son is near and dear. Sometimes the feeling may be stronger in favour of a perfect stranger than in that of a near kinsman. Thus an adopted son or a son purchased from a stranger would in many cases exclude daughters, brothers and such other near relations, not only in law but in the ideas and feelings of men. Owing to wide differences in principles and methods of social organisation therefore, there grows up very large differences in the schemes of kindred and of inheritance in different races.

MATRILINEAR AND PATRILINEAR SCHEMES OF DESCENT : Two main types may be easily distinguished, *viz.*, the matrilinear and patrilinear schemes. In matrilinear families, the normal type consists of males and females born in the house. The range of kindred as well as notions of nearness of relationship therefore are strictly limited to groups connected through females. On the contrary in patrilinear families kinship is counted generally through males, for the family consists of males born in the family and females brought into the family by marriage. Matrilinear kindred include brothers, sister's son, mother's brother, mother's sister, mother's sister's son and so on. Patrilinear kindred include son, natural or artificial, brothers, grand-father, etc., and their male descendants.

In a matrilinear family we should expect to find kinship strictly limited to children born of women born in the family. But in point of fact most matrilinear societies represent somewhat mixed types, in which children of the deceased himself have some share. The fact is that most societies of this character that we know of have partially passed out of the purely matrilinear stage and many of them have developed proprietary forms of marriage, though matrilinear kinship still adheres to them. As a result of this transition the law of succession in most such societies is not purely matrilinear.

MEAGRENESS OF THE OLD LAW OF SUCCESSION : Before I pass on to illustrations of the various rules of succession, I should like to refer to one interesting feature of the law of succession not merely of matrilinear but also of many patrilinear societies at an early stage and that is that the rules about succession do not follow lines of kinship very far. One, two or three small classes of heirs are named perhaps and there the law stops. Sometimes, the law expressly states that after that the kindred take the inheritance. This is the rule in the case of all savage societies. In ancient patriarchal societies also we find the same thing. Thus Gautama's list of enumerated heirs terminates with sons and appointed daughter's son and after that follows a comprehensive rule, "those connected by *pinda, gotra* and *rishi*, or the wife." This, with the exception of the wife, agrees remarkably with the law of the *Twelve Tables* where after the *Sui* come the *proximus agnatus*, after whom the property goes to the *gens*. Barring the reference to some relations through females, which has given rise to some controversy, the Germanic laws also are very similar.

All this indicates a stage in which the social mind is not yet up to the effort to think out a long line of heirs about whom questions may arise only rarely. Customs get established only with reference to cases which frequently occur, the rest is left to be settled as each case arises, by the proper authorities, the medicine man of the savages, the priests of the Aryan races or the *Parishads* in India. That is one reason why the early law is so little particular about settling the claims of the remoter heirs. Besides, primitive and ancient communities do not carry their ideas of relative strength of kinship very far. A certain number of near kindred such as the *sui* of Rome who are practically associated with one in the same household are distinguished from the rest by the recognition of a stronger bond of kinship. For the rest, the whole lot of kinsmen are on the same footing. They are all brothers, uncles, etc., of the deceased. Fine distinctions between them by counting the degrees of kindred is a discovery of a later age and a subtler mind.

The fact that the entire kindred—the whole settlement, takes the estate left by the deceased after very near kindred is often put forward as evidence of primitive community of ownership. It is suggested that the individual was only a limited owner and the property belonged to the kindred as a whole. The individual property gradually developed, but the communal ownership survived in the theory of the ultimate succession of the *gens* or clan.

I have put forward reasons to doubt the existence of communal ownership as the primary fact. If my view is correct, then the ultimate heirship of the clan or *gens* does not in any way reduce the force of those arguments. For it is quite conceivable that a rule like this might have developed out of individual ownership and individual rights of succession without assuming communal ownership.

EVOLUTION OF A LAW OF INHERITANCE : Let us imagine a time when landed property did not exist and all the wealth of the deceased consisted of his personal belongings. The primitive idea with regard to these seems to have been to bury these things with the deceased. In many retarded societies and in the primitive history of races we find illustrations of all the belongings of the deceased being buried with him, including his slaves, his wife or his favourite animals who were killed to accompany him for service to the deceased in the other world. In the state of society to which this idea primarily belongs there is and can be no law of inheritance. The deceased is not dead but continues his existence in some form under the ground and he takes his belongings with him. Gradually however, probably as society becomes richer and the faith in the continued existence after death exactly as during life becomes weakened, we find this necessity of burying everything with the deceased got round. One of the devices by which this is done is to bury with the deceased worthless substitutes of valuable articles while the originals are retained by his family. Another device was a donation *mortis causa* or otherwise during the lifetime of the deceased or, a distribution amongst sons or such near kindred,[1] so that when the man dies he has no property to go with him. As we have seen, it is probable that a custom of inheritance may have grown out of this practice. Another way in which the custom may have been developed is suggested by the right of the nearest kinsmen in some communities to take one or more of the belongings of the deceased. Whatever may be the exact origin of the law of inheritance, we find no evidence, nor is there any reason to suppose, that the first rule of inheritance was not a rule of individual succession. The heir, when he came to be recognised as such, was recognised as an individual. A law of inheritance is found to have been developed, with reference to personal property, on a purely

1 It is quite true that such donations are liable to be set aside at the optton of the heir in some societies. In Babylon the heir could get back properties given away by the deceased on payment of certain prices. But these are institutions of a later age, when a law of heirship has been established so far that the heir is supposed to have a sort of vested interest in the property.

individual basis, before land is recognised as property. In this law the kindred succeed as heir and not by virtue of any residuary ownership.

DIVERSITIES IN MATRILINEAR SOCIETIES : The actual rules of inheritance in matriarchal societies are as much diversified almost as among patriarchal societies. This is partly due to the more or less powerful influence exercised on these societies by the developing concept of ownership in wives and children, but in part, even apart from such influence, from the fact that even in matrilinear society kinship is viewed differently in different communities, doubtless owing to the fact of differences in social organisations. The result of these influences is a largely diversified order of succession in different societies organised on a matrilinear basis. To some extent again the order of succession is affected by a distinction between kinds of property. The reasons which underlie such differentiation are various. The relative importance of the different kinds of properties in the eyes of the community accounts for some of the difference. Others are accounted for by the source of the wealth. Property coming from the bride's father is treated differently from that coming from one's own ancestor. The utility of things to the particular persons concerned is another circumstance of importance. All these circumstances affect the order of succession to the property.

TUBE-TUBES : I should like to give here some illustrations of the diversities of the law of inheritance in matrilinear societies. Among the Tube-tube tribes of New Guinea one class of properties, including drums, lime-posts, lime spatulæ and canoes go to the sister's children and, if they are girls, they take for the benefit of their children. If the sister has no children the property passes to the maternal uncle, with a reversion at his death to a man's own brothers and sisters. This gives us a purely matrilinear order of succession. Property of the second category, such as arms, shells and the like, and also pigs, is divided between a man's own children and those of his sister. This discloses the introduction of the germs of patrilinear kinship. It will be noticed that the distinction in the kinds of property are founded on the relative importance of the articles.

WAGA-WAGAS AND BATHONGA : Among the Waga-waga tribes, ornaments given to a wife by a husband are regarded at his death as the heritage of his *gariauna*, a man who performs certain ceremonies at his grave. Among the Bathonga, of the two *assegais* which are a part of a man's regular equipment, the larger passes to the son, and the other to the uterine nephew. Here we notice that the son has acquired a position of superior importance, but the original matrilinear character of the kindred survives in the nephew, who, it is noticeable, has formally the choice between the *assegai*, though by custom he is bound to give the better one to the son.

But there are diversities in the rules of inheritance among matriarchal communities quite independently of these disturbing circumstances. Thus we find that while the sister's son and daughter, uterine brother and sister, maternal uncle, maternal aunt's son and daughter are regarded as heirs, they are not all heirs in every society, and their relative positions vary very much.

ORDER OF PREFERENCE OF HEIRS IN PATRIARCHAL SOCIETIES : In patriarchal societies, the normal order of succession would be to male kinsmen strictly in the male line. But who is the kinsman entitled to succeed in the first instance ? Generally speaking the son. But this is by no means the universal rule. There are traces of a rule of succession of brothers or other senior members of the family in preference to sons in some places. This rule known in Irish Law as tanistry, is found not only in Brehon laws of Ireland but in many other places, notably with reference to hereditary offices in unsettled times.[1] There are texts in Hindu law also which indicate that a rule of succession of brothers in preference to son apparently prevailed at some time in some Aryan communities in India in ancient times.

POSITION OF SONS : Even with regard to sons there is nothing like uniformity in the law of succession at different places. There is the rule of primogeniture by which the eldest son succeeds to the exclusion of younger children. On the contrary there are rules of ultimogeniture in some places by which

1. See Maine, *Early Institutions*, Lecture VII.

the youngest son succeeds to the exclusion of the elder brothers. But the general rule is that of division of the inheritance among the sons of the deceased. Even here however, we find that the partition is not necessarily equal. In many places we find the elder sons distinguished in some form or other. An extra share of the inheritance or some specific properties are very often given to the eldest son as his birth-right or under other pretences. Sometimes the preference takes the shape of a graduated scale in the case of all the elder brothers to the exclusion of the youngest. Very often sons take as such, irrespective of the status of their mothers. In many places, on the other hand, distinctions are made between sons with reference to the status or class of the mother, or the form or marriage or concubinage out of which the son is born. And, further complications are introduced by the introduction of artificial or secondary sons who do not all take equally.

These diversities in the law are determined by varying social environments. At the present stage of our knowledge it is not possible to construct anything like a general course of evolution of these various forms of the law. We can only indicate tendencies and certain consequences that seem to follow from certain circumstances.

PRIMOGENITURE : It seems that primogeniture was the general rule with regard to inheritance in patriarchal societies in which joint families continued after the father's death. The preferential treatment given to the eldest son was a survival of primogeniture. Maine, on the contrary, supposes primogeniture to have been originally associated with inheritance to offices and presumably a later development. As opposed to this theory we have the ancient Indian view reiterated in religious as well as the secular law that the eldest son takes the place of the father. In the sacral law of India the obsequies of the deceased are performed by the eldest son alone. This matches exactly with the view put forward in several texts of the law, whose age it is imposible to determine, that the eldest son takes the entire inheritance and the others live under him just as they lived under the father. In justification of this ancient law Indian authors are apt to refer to texts of religious law which lay down that a man is saved from the evils of sonlessness by the birth of the first son, the other sons being for spiritual purposes. more or less useless.

This law presupposes a condition of society in which families find it convenient to live together even after the death of the head, as for instance when enemies surround a family and there is therefore great need for cohesion within the family. It is proper also to a stage of society in which the wealth of the family is small. As families grow prosperous and society settles down in peace, the strength of the forces making for cohesion is reduced and a great disruptive force is introduced by the increased wealth. When such a state of society comes into existence, brothers tend to separate and custom of partition tends to grow up. Adventitious circumstances also may tend to promote separation, such as, for instance, the encouragement of priestly classes who promote the belief, as in India, that in partition there is increase of religious merit owing to the multiplication of sacrifices performed.

When separation becomes inevitable, the younger sons do not share equally with the eldest. The eldest gets some preference which grows less and less as time goes on. In India the several stages can be clearly marked. At first the eldest son is entitled to a double share, that is, what have been the father's share if he had chosen to make a partition during his life-time. But later on, we find that one-twentieth of the whole estate and the most valuable article out of the belongings of the father were reserved for the eldest son. By an analogical extension of this doctrine of the preference of the eldest-born son, later law provides for the preferential shares of the second and third sons as well. Ultimately however even this preference gave way and we find as early and author as Apastamba laying down that all sons took the property equally.

Ultimogeniture : Ultimogeniture belongs to a far earlier stage of society and it only survives in out-of-the-way places under completely changed circumstances. In the earliest days of patriarchal societies everywhere and demonstrably in India, joint families of father and grown-up sons were unknown. Each son as he grew up separated from the family and set up home for himself. The youngest son who was generally too young to leave the house, being a member of the house therefore took the inheritance. That is how ultimogeniture conceivably originated in some societies. But the identical institution may have arisen under quite different circumstances. In England for instance the ultimogeniture of the Borough English tenure seems to have grown up out of a system of equal division under the influence of the feudal notion of the one tenant for one land.[1] In a modified form we find the institution in the Roman Law and Hindu Law where the *sons*, as distinguished from the *emancipatus*, and the son born after partition take in preference to the other sons in the succession to the father's share after his death.

LEGITIMATE AND SECONDARY SONS : Sonship belongs in most systems of law to the child of the lawfully wedded wife. The Aryan law was apparently very particular about it. Marriage was a religious institution amongst Aryans and constituted a partnership in religion between the husband and wife. The child borne by such a wife was apparently the only son recognised in the earliest times. The evidence of Roman, Greek, Germanic and early Vedic law seems to coincide on this head. In Babylon on the contrary the rule of legitimacy was by no means so rigorous and not only was the succession open to the son of the concubine and slave as well as to that of the wife, but even the preference due to the eldest son was given to the son first born no matter by what woman.

GROWTH OF SECONDARY SONS IN INDIA : But the law is seen to undergo various changes under the pressure of social environments. In India we find a remarkable history of evolution of the law on this head. While the *Vedas* refuse to recognise a son other than one begotten on a lawfully wedded wife, the *Smritis* gradually recognise several kinds of secondary sons, including the son of an appointed daughter, the son begotten by *Niyoga* and a variety of other sons most of whom are bastards born in the family. The earlier law books distinguish between these secondary sons and give the right to inherit to one set but exclude the other from it altogether. In course of time however all these clases of persons rise to the

1 Pollock and Maitland, *Op. cit.* Vol. II, p. 280.

rank of sons and are given the right to succeed to the properties of the deceased on the failure of legitimate issue.

It is difficult to offer any definite suggestion as to the exact circumstances which led to this retrogression. It is quite clear that a comparatively small population of Aryans surrounded by alien communities on all sides felt the need for as many sons as possible. It is possible also that the customs of the surrounding communities exercised a profound influence on the Aryan society in the matter of their social institutions. The period during which the development occurred was one of most restless activity on the part of the Aryans in their effort to adapt themselves to their new environments. The rigours of the old laws had therefore to yield before the pressure of social needs and the license of a new life.

But the reaction came later and we notice the twelve kinds of sons evaporating almost under our eyes, leaving as their residue the adopted and the arrogated son, to describe them by their Roman names. The old law is not repealed or abrogated, it simply dies out as the social need for the license in the matter of sons disappears and the Aryan bias in favour of legitimacy reasserts itself. Other distinctions now force themselves on our attention. Even with regard to legitimate sons distinctions spring up according as the son is born of a wife of the same caste or lower caste, according as the mother was married according to the approved or the disapproved rites. All these distinctions grow more and more rigorous till we find marriage outside the caste practically abolished and forms of marriage other than *Brahma* and *Asura* altogether discarded.

CHAPTER XIII

THE LAW OF DESCENT—(*Contd.*)

I.—The Succession of Agnates

In a strictly patriarchal society, after the son the agnates would take the property, and the nearest agnates would be the brothers.

We have seen that the brother in some exceptional cases takes precedence over the son, but in most societies brothers follow the sons. Among brothers there would be grounds of distinction according as he was full or half-brother, and as he was either joint or separate.

ORIGINALLY THE ENTIRE KINDRED INHERITED : It seems that in many cases the original idea was that the entire kindred took the inheritance of a sonless man. The idea of distinguishing between different grades of agnates is comparatively late. When this is recognised however the way in which the proximity is worked out is far from identical in different patriarchal societies or even in the societies of the Aryan stock.

EARLIEST INDIAN LAW RELATING TO SUCCESSION OF AGNATES : The most ancient law relating to the inheritance of collaterals and ascendants among Aryans is, as has been pointed out before, extraordinarily meagre and gives us no guidance in working out the scheme of succession in detail. I have already mentioned the scheme of inheritance in the *Twelve Tables* and *Gautama Dharmasutra*. Vasistha gives the following scheme for succession : (*i*) The first six kinds of sons ; (*ii*) *Sapindas* and the second group of secondary sons ; (*iii*) Spiritual teacher or pupil, and (*iv*) The king, Baudhayana, also gives practically the same list with the exception that after *sapindas* he inserts *sakulyas*. Gautama is distinguished from these in so far as he would give the wife the custody of the inheritance if she wishes to have a son by *Niyoga*. Later on, Indian law gets more complicated.

A few points may be noted with reference to these statements of the law. In the first place the inheritance passes on strictly agnatic lines. It is quite true that the term *sapinda* is ambiguous, but there is no doubt that although this term included daughter's sons and other cognates in later times, in its origin the term was strictly confined to agnates. With regard to the others, the *sakulyas* and *sagotras*, of course, there is no doubt that they are always agnates. Secondly, we note that these statements of the law differ as regards the exact agnates who may take.

It may possibly be inferred from this that in the kernel of the law out of which these variations were evolved there was no definite provision about it. What it probably provided was that the agnates, or rather all the kindred or, at best, the whole of a class of kindred such as *sapinda* or *sakulya* as a body succeeded. The rules as to the relative priority as between individual kinsmen belonging to the same class by reason of nearness of relationship were worked out in detail in later times. The result of this process was an enumeration of a certain number of heirs in succession followed by a succession of *sapindas*, *sakulyas* or other more distant kindred by classes, the relative priority of each individual being determined by reference to certain rules of counting degrees of proximity.

THE DEVELOPMENT OF THE LAW IN ROME, GREECE AND IRELAND : In Rome also the development of the law was apparently similar. The *proximus agnatus* was distinguished in the first instance and the relative proximity determined by counting the generations. At Athens succession lists proceeded on the basis of a classification which resembled some of the schools in Hindu Law. In the absence of the lineal descendants of the deceased, the inheritance went to a class of very near kindred called the *αγχιστεια* extending not beyond the children of his first cousins. The next class were descendants of the paternal grand-father. After these are found interposed, the descendants and collaterals of the mother, after which remoter kinsmen succeed according to proximity. Apart from the introduction of matrilinear kinsmen, which we shall consider later, this scheme of succession gives us an order which is an effort to develop the original rule of succession of kindred without any definite principle of differentiation. A very similar result was achieved in the same attempt by the Celtic laws. In Ireland after the descendants there came a group of kinsmen (*gelfine*) within four degrees from the father. Next came the *derbfine* who were descendants within four degrees of the grand-father. The *iaifine* included similar descendants of the great-grand-father and the *indfine* who came next included similar relations of the great-great-grand-father.

THE LAW OF GERMANIC RACES : Among Germanic races a somewhat different development seems to have occurred in so far as matrilinear kinship is concerned. According to Tacitus, on the failure of children his next of kin inherit ; "his own brothers, those of his father, or those of his mother." In the *Lex Salica* after the sons and daughters come the mother, the borther and the sister, the mother's sister and in some of the codes the father's sister. The father is not an heir except in the later law. The *Lex Ribuaria* and the other *Leges Barbarorum* also agree in the main with this except in so far as the father and the father's sister and father's brother are counted as heirs. It is noticeable that in tho oldest *Salic* code females are altogether excluded from inheritance. Still, this preference of mother's relations is a circumstance which wants explanation.

PARENTELIC SCHEME IN ANGLO-SAXON LAW : It is remarkable however that in the Anglo-Saxon law and the English law evolved from it we miss this element altogether and find a law of succession by classes not altogether dissimilar to the Irish Law. This is the parentelic scheme. By a person's *parentela* we understand a person's descendants how low soever. In the parentelic scheme of succession which we find fully developed in the English law of the thirteenth century, on the failure of the descendants of a person the inheritance went to the *parentela* of his father and failing that to the *parentela* of his grand-father and so backwards in the ascending line. The question of the antiquity of this parentelic scheme in England is shrouded in obscurity. It cannot have dated back to pre-ethnic times or even to the days of Anglo-

Saxons in their German home. As elsewhere, this scheme seems to have been evolved in the effort to work out a scheme of succession for the more distant kindred.

II.—Women as Heirs

WOMEN NOT HEIRS IN PATRIARCHAL SOCIETY : In a strictly agnatic scheme of succession, women or children of the women born in the family have no place. Wives are not heirs, because in a rigorously patriarchal family they are always to be kept under subjection. Daughters are not heirs because they go out of the family and their children are children of a different family altogether. But sooner or later, every patriarchal family develops cognatic kinship and in most places widows are recognised as heirs. The problem of the transition from the purely patriarchal to this modified view of heirship has not yet been definitely solved.

THE POSITION OF THE WIDOW : There seems to have been a time in most patriarchal societies when the wife, far from being regarded as an heir of the husband, was herself looked upon as a valuable part of the assets of the husband. The heir in many places inherited the wives of the deceased along with his other properties, barring his own mother. At other places we find the wives distributed amongst the kinsmen, a preference being given to the husband's brother. The *Levirate* of the Semitic races would seem to be a considerably modified development out of this institution. The taking of the wife of the deceased involved certain obligations. If the deceased had died sonless, for instance, it implied that the first son of the widow would be considered as the son of the deceased. I have said before, how this leads, as the next step, to the *Niyoga* of ancient India, which, as we shall presently see, had an important bearing on the wife's position as heir in Hindu law.

Among Aryan races, the evidence points unmistakeably to the evolution of a much higher view of womanhood. The position of the *materfamilias* in Rome and the *grihapatni* in India was a remarkably dignified one. The primitive Aryan marriage was a religious contract, absolutely monogamous, by which the wife entered into spiritual and domestic partnership with the husband. Tacitus's meagre description of the position of women in Germanic society also seems to indicate a position of very great importance for the wife.

THE WIDOW'S RIGHT OF INHERITANCE EVOLVED—(A) FROM THE PRACTICE OF MAKING GIFTS : At the same time, the wife is not recognised as heir in the most ancient stratum of Hindu law or in Greek, Roman or Germanic laws. The position of the Hindu widow in the *Rig Vedic* times is very obscure. The *Grihya* law indicates that the domestic rituals terminates when the husband has been cremated with the *Grihya* fire. So the theory of the continuation of the existence of the husband in the wife which we find in later law could not have existed at this stage. The result was that if a man died sonless, the house absolutely broke up, and the widow became a dependant on his kinsmen. On the contrary quite an early tradition, though not as early perhaps as that embodied in the *Grihya* law, records the case of a husband dividing his wealth equally between his two wives preliminary to his retirement to the woods. This it may be noted was not yet a rule of inheritance, it was in the nature of a gift by the husband, and it is not improbable that, in some Aryan societies in India at any rate, the sonless wife's right to inherit may have developed out of a practice of the husband to give the property to the wife during his lifetime.

AND (B) FROM NIYOGA : That this was not the universal source of the wife's right to inherit is indicated by the text of Gautama, which is undoubtedly the earliest statement of the law on the subject. Gautama gives the inheritance to the *sapindas*, *sagotras*, etc., and lays down as an alternative that the widow should seek to raise issue to her husband by *Niyoga*. The brief *sutra* does not say in so many words that if the wife seeks to raise offspring by *Niyoga* she has custody of the heritage till the son is born, but that was obviously the meaning of the rule. In any case, it obviously led to that conclusion. In later books we find the question of the wife's rights hotly debated. Some contend that the wife's right originates in her capacity to raise issue to the deceased by *Niyoga*. Against this, others contend that *Niyoga* is not admissible if it is prompted by the desire for the inheritance. Both sides have more or less old texts to cite in their favour.

The position, historically, seems to have been this. When *Niyoga* became common in *Arya* society as a mode of raising an heir to the deceased, the widow engaged in the *Niyoga* naturally had the custody of the property until the son was born. The time during which women had the inheritance might be long or short,—she might never have a son. In this way people became habituated to the idea of widows continuing in possession of the property after the husband's death and gradually in their being recognised as preferential heirs. But on behalf of the kinsmen whose expectations were thus baulked limitations and restrictions came to be imposed upon the widow's right. The injunction seeking to prevent *Niyoga* for the sake of the inheritance is one form of the attempt at restraint. A different form of restraint is represented by the rule that the widow takes only a life interest in the property inherited from the husband without any power of alienation. This rule could only have arisen when the heirship of the widow is established beyond a doubt and, in point of fact we find it referred to only in later law books.

It is possible that the right of the widow may have grown up gradually. There are texts of law which indicate that the widow takes the inheritance in lieu of her subsistence, and a theory which survived till very late times, that the widow takes the inheritance if the property is small and just enough for her maintenance, can possibly trace an ancient pedigree. But these unworkable limitations were swept away in course of time and we find the later *Dharmasâstras* recognising the widow's right to inherit without restraint. Kâtyâyana who is about the latest of *Dharmasâstra*-writers bases the widow's right on her position well-recognised in the sacred law, that the wife is half the person of the husband and continues his existence after his death. That this was the latest development of law cannot be doubted, but the text indicates that, throughout, the religious law, which gave the wife a very lofty position, exercised a considerable influence in determining this final development. The changed order of society and the consequent change of the outlook of people towards the widow acted as the motive force behind the entire development.

Patriarchal society was not likely to be stable anywhere except under conditions and ideas which prevailed in very ancient times. With the change in this, society gradually broke through the strictly patriarchal system in many ways. One of these was the change of outlook towards women. Women are gradually viewed less and less as chattels and come to be regarded more and more as companions and equals of men. A concomitant of this change is the improvement in the status of wives. It is achieved in different ways in different countries, but a very general result of this improved status is the heirship of the wife. In Rome the progress of the wife to full heirship was slow and tardy though the *materfamilias* was a person of very great importance, because perhaps, the wife was generally very well provided for otherwise. In England, under the feudal law the wife's dower was a limited right, because the entire constitution of the feudal system militated against her rights. Occasionally too the progress has been retarded for a time by a wave of reaction conditioned by new social circumstances. But the general tendency has been everywhere in patriarchal society, sooner or later, to give the sonless wife the right of inheritance to her husband's property.

DAUGHTER AND COGNATES AS HEIRS : I have already dealt with the history of the introduction of the daughter and the daughter's son and through them the entire body of cognates into the Hindu scheme of kinship. The right of inheritance went with kinship as a matter of course. In Rome, cognation was deliberately introduced by the Prætor as a part of the *Jus Naturale*. But before the institution could have risen to the rank of a natural law in the estimation of *jurisconsults* it must have established itself already in the mind of the people. It was because the patriarchal organisation of society had given way so far that married daughters had often come to live with their parents—and sonless people would have their daughters about them—that it could seem unnatural to people that a daughter's son of a sonless man should never have the inheritance. The conditions under which cognation came to be recognised in Greece and Rome were not identical with those in India, but behind such recognition everywhere there were changed social institutions which made it possible for affection to extend to married daughters and their children and for daughters not to be made altogether alien by marriage.

SUPPOSED TRACES OF MOTHER-RIGHT IN GERMANIC SOCIETY : Germanic law however is not capable of explanation on this basis. Tacitus mentions that in Germany children are regarded as kindered to paternal and maternal uncles alike. This of course is perfectly intelligible. This implies that the principle of cognation was recognised here to a greater extent than elsewhere, but it does not interfere with a theory of the original patriarchal character the social organisation.

The difficulty arises however from the obvious preference shown to maternal kindred in the *Barbarian* codes. In the earliest code of the *Lex Salica*, females are altogether excluded, but still the mother's brother comes before the father's brother. In later law the same preference of maternal kinsmen is retained. The father is not regarded as an heir at all in most of these codes and he is not an heir under Anglo-Saxon law, though the mother is everywhere regarded as heir.

The exclusion of the father is easily accounted for. In early Germanic society, even in early Anglo-Saxon law the son could not conceivably become owner of any appreciable property during the father's life-time. So the case of a father succeeding his son was hardly conceivable in those days. This therefore does not imply mother-right or any deviation from the patriarchal idea in family organisation.

The preference shown for the maternal aunt and the maternal uncle over the paternal aunt and paternal uncle however is not so easily explained. Opinion in German learned circles is overwhelmingly in favour of considering these as survivals of *Mutterrecht* which, according to them, prevailed amongst Germans. The arguments advanced in support of this view are by no means convincing. The pre-eminence given to sons above all other heirs in all the *Barbarian* codes go entirely against the mother-right theory. And, there can be no doubt of the patriarchal character of the society in Germany of primitive times from collateral evidence. The husband, according to Tacitus, had complete control over the wife ; the wife lived with the husband and was expected to be scrupulously chaste. Although father-right as such is not vouched for by Tacitus, the evidences in favour of the father's power derived from collateral sources are not wanting. All these things, taken along with evidences of the original institutions of the Aryan race seems to place the thesis about mother-right on a very doubtful plane, to say the least.

The mere preference of mother's kindred in a scheme of inheritance, specially where the preference is only slight, may be explained otherwise. Influence of communities among whom Germanic races may have lived and developed their institutions, may account for the rule. Besides, strict exogamy appears to have been abrogated quite early by the Germans. Where the mother's kindred are not aliens to the kin but a part of them, the treatment of relations through the father and the mother on the same footing would be quite natural. If we consider further, that a father might have more than one wife, the possibility of the mother being intimately associated with her own kin and her son showing preference for the mother's kindred is quite conceivable. In fact the utmost that we can say is that we cannot explain these rules. We do not know enough of the social history and environments of the Germanic race to say how these institutions so peculiar in a race of the Indo-Germanic stock may have come into existence.

CHAPTER XIV

TESTAMENTARY SUCCESSION

TESTAMENTUM COMITIAE CALATIIS : Sir Henry Maine's theory about the history of wills is entirely based upon the history of testaments in Roman law. The early will of Roman law was the *Testamentum Comitiæ Calatiis*. The *Comitia Calata* was an assembly of all the *gentes*, indentical in constitution with the *Comitia Curiata* but performing different functions. It was an assembly in which all the patricians were present and which was in a special manner under religious protection. The institution of an heir by a patrician in this Assembly was a solemn and formal act which was absolutely binding.

Maine is right in insisting that the true meaning of this testament must not be sought in the fact that the *Comitia Calata* was originally the legislative body of Rome and that this declaration confirmed by the *Comitia* was in effect a legislative modification of the law of inheritance. Such a theory is untenable, because the *Comitia Curiata* was never a legislative body in the modern sense, and if there was a general law of inheritance in sacred law which did not recognise the testament, the *Comitia* could not conceivably alter the law. Maine's own view is that the significance of the declaration in the *Comitia* lay in the fact that all the *gentes* were present there. It implies according to him that under the primitive Roman law, testaments were only permissible on the failure of heirs and this declaration ensured that the testament deprived no one of the inheritance without his consent.

THE ROOT OF THIS FORM OF TESTAMENT IN INSTITUTIONS ANTERIOR TO A LAW OF INHERITANCE : When a law of intestate succession has been definitely settled, ancient law often shows itself jealous of dispositions of property to the detriment of the interests of heirs. This tendency manifests itself in rules restricting alienations *inter vivos* as well as testamentary, in the provision of a birthright of a *legitim* and occasionally in forbidding altogether dispositions of property so as to affect the law of inheritance. But as we have seen before, the power of disposing of property in such a manner that the gift should continue to be binding after death, already existed before a definite rule of inheritance and the heir's right to succeed came to be recognised. No doubt this right was exercised in most places by an act *inter vivos* but in many places the gift was *mortis causa* and, in India, it was in effect more in the nature of a testamentary disposition than aught else, for the donor, in such cases, retired from the world for life after making the gift. The testamentary gift of Rome may easily have developed out of this and, for placing the title of the successor beyond cavil, it may have been made in the presence of the entire community. It is nothing unusual in ancient times to have important juristic acts affecting the status of persons performed in the presence of the entire kindred or community. Thus Vasistha insists that an adoption must be made after sacrifices made, in the presence of all the kindred and with notice to the king. In the *Njal Saga* we find that when Unna wishes to sever the marriage tie with Hrut, she goes and makes the declaration on the Hill of Laws, at the Thing, the assembly of the entire community periodically convened for transacting legal business.

THE MANCIPATORY WILL OF LATER ROMAN LAW PRESUPPOSES THE IDEA OF TESTATION : If this view is correct the testament will have to be traced back to its source in the same act of primitive law out of which the law of intestate succession was evolved. The supposition that rules of intestate succession were first established and that testaments arose out of the discontent people felt at a later age with the law of inheritance cannot then be sustained. In attempting to establish this thesis Maine entirely slurs over the testament in the *Comitia Calata* and puts exclusive emphasis on the Mancipatory Will in Roman law. It is quite true that the Mancipatory Will was historically the source of the Roman Will of later days, but it did not introduce the idea of testation for the first time in Roman society. On the contrary the idea was already in existence from the earliest historical times in the shape of the testament in the *Comitia Calata*. The Mancipatory Will was evolved much later for almost the identical reasons which led to the evolution of coemption as a form of marriage. The testament in the *Comitia Calata* was open only to the Patricii. The Plebeian also wanted to make his will. He knew what a will was, there was no difficulty about making a will except that there was no recognised legal form of will which a Plebeian might adopt. The whole question with him was to find a form for doing in effect what the Patrician was already doing. The same problem arose when the Plebeian wanted to have a *justum matrimonium* with the consequent rights over the wife and children. And a solution was obtained by recourse to the same institution of Mancipation which had by this time been made quite handy for the purpose by the development of fiduciary Mancipation. The evolution of the Mancipatory Will therefore furnishes no clue to the origin of the Will as such. It presupposed the existence of the concept of testation. In Rome this concept dates back to the earliest historical times. It is possible to trace back its history by reference to the customs and laws of ancient and retarded races till it shades off imperceptibly into a transfer *inter vivos*. It does not appear that in primitive society when property consisted of small personal belongings, people found any difficulty in understanding the disposition of properties by a dying man as he chose. In Anglo-Saxon law testamentary gifts of land seem to have been practised without the people being conscious of doing anything out of the way or of developing of a new category of law. So far as I am aware the power of testament is nowhere recognised in the written laws of the Anglo-Saxons ; but it was practised without question before the Norman conquest.

LATER HISTORY OF WILLS IN ROME : The later history of Wills in Roman Law is interesting as illustrating the circuitous processes by which people achieve what are to us simple results ; it does not illustrate the evolution of the testamentary idea. When the Plebeian wanted a Will, Roman jurists adapted the Mancipation for the purpose. The entire *familia*, the sum-total of the rights and obligations was passed on to the *Familiæ Emptor* under an obligation imposed by the *nuncupatio*, to let the testator remain in possession of the properties during his lifetime and to dispose of the properties after his death according to the directions of the testator. As, by the law of the *Twelve Tables*, the directions in the *nuncupatio* had become binding in law, this had the effect of transferring property so that the transfer should take effect after the death of the testator. Later on, the formalities were dropped in due course and all that remained of the Mancipatory Will was a declaration attested by seven witnesses, representing the *Familiæ Emptor*, the *Libripens* and the five witnesses who were present at a Mancipatory Will. Thus was developed the Prætorian Will which was the first Will in the modern sense. The Mancipatory Will, by its comparative simplicity of procedure gradually ousted the Will in the *Comitia Calata* and was established as the only form of Will for the Plebeian and the Patrician alike.

RESTRICTIONS ON POWERS OF TESTATION : When a law of intestate succession has been established, the heir, in course of time, is looked upon as having a sort of vested right in the inheritance and there grows up a tendency to restrain the owner's power to make gifts or other dispositions of property which would deprive the heir of his expectations. The later history is a struggle between this tendency and the theory of freedom of disposition. The result of this conflict is a compromise which takes various shapes.

I have already said how the rights of a Hindu owner in the matter of the disposition of his properties were gradually restrained by law till the culmination was reached in one school of law in the recognition of equal rights of the regular heir in the property in the hands of a person. We find restraints on gifts in other forms in other places. Amongst some races we find that when a man makes a gift of property the donee's title may be set aside at the donor's death, by his heirs. In Babylon, where the deceased has alienated property during his lifetime his heirs may have the sale set aside on payment of the price paid by the assignee. In Hindu Law one of the earlier restrictive rules only seeks to prevent the alienation of the entire ancestral property so as to leave the heirs altogether without a subsistence. This sort of rule is found to develop into rules which provide a *legitim* for the heir in the shape of a definite aliquot part of the property.

CIRCUMSTANCES AFFECTING THE DEVELOPMENT OF WILLS : The ultimate effect of this struggle between the principles of alientation and the vested rights of heirs is determined by a great many social factors. In Rome we find a free power of testation developed in all things, subject to the heir's *legitim*. On the contrary, in India, we find the testamentary power could never develop beyond the power of making a partition at will among sons by an act *inter vivos*. The reasons for this difference have to be sought in the social and legal environments of the institution. In Rome not only is the power of testation recognised, the people display a passion for testaments. This goes along with an wooden and rigorous law of inheritance which preferred very distant agnates and gentiles to near relations like daughter's sons and sister's sons and uterine cousins. This narrow law of inheritance and the law of wills acted and reacted on each other. The law of inheritance gave rise to the freedom of testation. And, the freedom of testation, coupled with freedom of adoption took away the incentive to a reform in the law of inheritance. In Rome the change in the law of inheritance came very slowly, and, even when cognates were recognised as heirs, they had at first to take a very subordinate place in the scheme of inheritance.

In India on the contrary the law of inheritance is found to be more elastic and more responsive to the changes in social relations. This perhaps accounts in certain measure for the fact that testaments never developed in India. Besides, there is the fact that the partition of the inheritance by an old man during his lifetime was evidently so much of a rule and such freedom was apparently permitted in the disposition in the earlier days of the law, that testamentary dispositions were not needed. In addition we have to take into consideration the fact that large families developed comparatively early in Hindu society and, even before the notion of joint family ownership developed, the family property must have come to be looked upon as more or less of a provision for the maintenance of the family. In large families there are comparatively few occasions when the family becomes extinct altogether. Besides, there was ample power in the owner to deprive any one of the inheritance or to distinguish any heir by giving him a preferential share *inter vivos*. All these circumstances must be responsible very largely for the absence of testamentary powers in Hindu Law.

ADOPTION AND WILLS : Besides, there was the institution of adoption, which to some extent served the same purpose as a will. That adoption became a very important legal institution in India in the middle ages owing, to some extent perhaps, to the growing inelasticity of the law of inheritance, cannot be doubted, and it is also clear that in many cases adoption serves a testamentary purpose. But there is some risk of attaching too much significance to this aspect of adoption. We must bear in mind that adoption was not a very favourite institution in ancient India. Besides even in later days when the law of adoption grew into huge proportions, it was resorted to, in more cases than not, for the purpose of provision of the soul's welfare in after life or from the natural craving for paternity or maternity. The testamentary purpose of adoption is not very prominent even in modern times ; and in most places there were very great difficulties in making the institution serve the purpose. For adoption only very young boys are admissible and very often they are not adopted by reason the particular boy being singled out in the affections of the adoptive parent. In adoption the point of importance is to have a son, identity of the son is secondary and tends to be immaterial ; while in testament the important thing is the person chosen.

APPENDIX

THE HINDU JOINT FAMILY

There is a large amount of confusion with regard to the law of joint family in ancient India. The general opinion among Western scholars from the time of Maine onwards has been that the *Mitâkshara* view of the constitution of the joint family and the rights of the members *inter se* is the primitive Hindu concept and that the view represented by the *Dâyabhâga* of Jimutavahana represents a later advance.

With regard to what the real law of the *Mitâkshara* is, there has also been some amount of confusion. A series of judicial decisions has, by drawing on the concept of the law of joint tenancy in English law, given an interpretation to the law which goes very much further than what is laid down in the *Mitâkshara* itself. The law of the *Mitâkshara* only amounts to this that the immovable property in the hands of a person is to be regarded as a fund for the maintenance of the family ; and his sons, grandsons and great-grandsons in the male line acquire a proprietary interest in it by birth. This co-ownership does not go so far as to entitle sons and grandsons to claim a partition against the will of the father. They have a right to partition, otherwise than at the will of the father, only against an old and senile father and where the father is suffering from a protracted illness, but not otherwise. The father, however, has no power to alienate the immovable property without the consent of the sons, grandsons and great-grandsons except for family necessity and for necessary religious purposes. Some distinction is made between self-acquired and ancestral properties in this respect.[1]

It can be said without hesitation that this was not the oldest law in India. In Vedic Society, it is evident, not only

---

1 Mitakshara, under Yajnavalkya II, 114, pp. 181-84 (Moghe's Ed.) This view was put forward with great force by Nelson. See his *View of Hindu Law* and *Prospectus on a Scientific Study of Hindu Law* and Burnell in his introduction to the *Dayabhaga*.

have the sons no right by birth in the immovable property in the hands of the father, but there was no such thing as a joint family of the father and grown-up sons. Heads of families in Vedic literature are found to make gifts of immovable properties quite freely and no suggestion of the sons having the right to forbid such alienations is even hinted at.[1] The absolute mastery of the father in the family over, not only the properties, but also the persons of sons in Vedic literature is not a whit inferior to that of the Roman *paterfamilias*.

The scheme of life of the *Arya* as evidenced by the *Grihya* and *Dharma Sutras* also negatives the idea of joint families in Vedic times. The *Arya* is initiated at a tender age, after which he lives with his teacher till he reaches maturity. After finishing his studies he performs a ceremonial ablution and becomes a *Snâtaka*. The life of a *Snâtaka* is one of only slightly less austerity than that of a *Brahmachâri* and his chief characteristic is that he has no fire at which he can offer his oblations. This idea would be inconsistent with the membership of a joint family which is conceived, at a later age, to be a family with one domestic fire (*Grihya Agni*) at which all the members offer their daily oblations.

The *Snâtaka* is enjoined to get himself married as soon as possible and to set up a fire. At the wedding, a fire is lighted, before which the ceremonies to be performed at the bride's father's house are performed. This fire is carefully carried in the bridal chariot to the bridegroom's house where it is established. And from that day onwards the married couple has to keep the fire constantly lighted and to offer daily oblations to it. Each marriage in the Vedic and *Grihya* ritual therefore means the lighting of a separate fire and each Hearth-Fire is the symbol of a separate house. The idea of one common fire for an entire household consisting of father and married sons and grandsons is a later concept and is inconsistent with the entire scheme of the *Grihya* ritualism. In later ritual, apparently when the perpetual Hearth-Fire has ceased to be a feature of the household, we find a common fire which is

1 Compare, for instance, the opening story of *Kathopanishad*, in which the king is found to give away all he had, though he has a son. Numerous such stories of gifts would be familiar to every student of Vedic Literature.

broken up with the lighting of separate fires on a partition. In the *Grihya* ritual however we do not find such a joint fire anywhere. The *Grihya* fire and *Grihya* rites of each married couple are throughout conceived as separate in the *Grihya Sutras*.

In this connection, it is worthy of note that the *Apastamba Grihya Sutras* interposes the ceremony of House-building between the nuptial ceremonies at the bride's house and those at the bridegroom's house. This seems to indicate clearly that the *Grihya* contemplated that a person built a house upon his marriage, before he brought home his wife.

Another fact which seems to lead to the same conclusion is the plan of a house as indicated in the ritual of *Baliharana* in Baudhâyana's *Grihya Sutras*. In this ceremony offerings are made at different parts of the householder's house. After the offering at the front gate of the house the worshipper "goes out" and makes his offering at the "eldest brother's house."[1] This obviously indicates that while brothers lived side by side, each brother had a separate house, including his bedroom, his fire-house, his store-room, his husking-room, etc. In the scheme of *Balis* to be offered we should have expected to have found reference to the rooms of other members of a joint household living within the ambit of the same house, if the existence of such joint households were contemplated as possible.

On the whole it can be said with confidence that there is no trace in the ritual literature of the Vedic times of joint families of married sons and grandsons living in the same house with the father. The Vedic family consisted of the husband, wife and immature sons and unmarried daughters.

The only evidence which may be urged against this view, so far as I have been able to find, is the text (*Rig Veda*, X, 85, 46) :

साम्राज्ञी श्वशुरे भव साम्राज्ञी श्वश्र्वां भव । ननान्दरि साम्राज्ञी भव साम्राज्ञी अधिदेवृषु ।

This passage is usually translated thus "Be empress over the father-in-law, be empress over the mother-in-law, be empress

[1] **उपनिष्क्रम्य ज्येष्ठावकाशे ।**—Bodh. Grihya.

over sisters-in-law. Be empress over the *devaras* (husband's brothers)."

In the first place I find difficulty in accepting this translation inasmuch as the interpretation of *samrâjni* in the *Rig Veda* as 'empress' seems to be an anachronism. I do not know of any unambiguous evidence in the *Rig Veda* to indicate that the concept of "Empire" was known in those days. It seems more probable that *samrâjni* in the *Rig Veda* stood for its radical sense of "specially agreeable" or "specially adorning." If we take this sense of the term this text would mean that the bride is invoked to be agreeable to the father-in-law, the mother-in-law and brothers and sisters-in-law. This would not necessarily involve their living in the same household. As we gather from the *Baliharana* ceremony in Baudhâyana's *Grihya*, though brothers, sons, etc., had separate houses, their houses lay side by side. As against others, they formed a distinct group living in adjoining houses and, together with other similar groups descended from a not too remote ancestors, they formed a wider group (the *kula* or the *gens*) and the groups gradually widened into societies of *gotra*, *jana*, *janma*, etc. If this is correct, the invocation can be easily understood without assuming that the relations referred to in this text necessarily lived in the same house. They were near one another and for many purposes they had common interests and a common life as distinguished from other members of the society, but they might, for all that, live in separate houses.

The joint family of the father and grown-up and married sons and grandsons of which we find plenty of evidence in the *Smritis* came into existence later on. The growth of this family probably coincided with growing prosperity and the importance of landed property. So long as land was abundant and one had only to settle on new land to start cultivation, a son on marriage naturally went out of the house and set up for himself. At a later date, when the land could not be had for the asking, the family land would attract the sons and they would not separate so easily. This and other circumstances probably contributed to build up the joint family. How far this development was the natural result of economic forces and how far it was determined by extraneous influences will never be exactly known.

In Vedic society, as I have mentioned above, there is no indication of the existence of the rights of the family in the properties, immovable or otherwise, in the hands of a person. In the extant *Dharmasastras* too we do not get any trace of any such right. On the contrary the idea underlying them is throughout the same as we find in Roman law—that of absolute individual ownership of the *paterfamilias*. It is quite true that the father in his old age was expected, as a matter of course, to divide his wealth among his sons (*Rig Veda* I, 70, 5 ; X, 61, 1. *Taitt. Samhita* III, 19, 4) but this did not apparently amount to a right of the sons to claim partition. Before partition between sons, the father was apparently absolute in his ownership.

In later law we find restraints on alienation growing. The texts of law bearing on the subject, which were doubtless developed in different stages of society and in different environments are an interesting study. They show a gradually growing tendency to restrain the father's free dealings with the property till at last we reach the climax in a theory of the acquisition of co-ownership with the father of sons and grandsons from the moment of their birth.

It is idle to seek to place these texts in a chronological order. For, apart from the fact that the chronology, even of extant complete *Smritis* is as hopeless a quest as any in archæology, the texts are mostly to be found surviving only in fragmentary quotations in the text-books of the middle ages. No attempt to place these fragments in a chronological order is therefore likely to be successful. Besides, even if the chronology of the texts could be ascertained, it would give no clue to the actual sequence of the texts in an evolutionary order. For the texts were composed in widely different lands in which the paces of development of laws were probably very different. A law or an institution which had been extinct in the Punjab for centuries might be flourishing in the Andhra country several centuries later. The mere fact, therefore, that a particular text was recorded in the Andhra country at a later date would not necessarily imply that it represented a later stage of law.

It is quite possible however to construct an evolutionary sequence in the texts if we remember that the earliest of these texts must be those which approximate nearest to the Vedic rule of absolute ownership of the father. From this point of view we can place the various texts in four different groups corresponding to four different stages in the evolution of the law.

In the first group we may place the texts denying any rights of sons; *e.g.*,

ऊर्द्ध्वं पितुश्च मातुश्च समेत्य भ्रातरः समम् ।
भजेरण् पैतृकं ऋकथमनीशास्ते हि जीवतोः ॥ Manu.

"Upon the demise of the father and the mother, the brothers should come together and divide the paternal wealth, they have no property in it while they (the parents) live."

पितर्य्युपरते पुत्राः विभजेयुर्द्धनं पितुः ।
अस्वाम्यं हि भवेदेषां निर्दोषे पितरि स्थिते ॥ Devala.

"Upon the death of the father, the sons should divide the wealth of the father; they have no property so long as the father lives faultless."

जीवति पितरि पुत्राणामर्थादान विसर्गाक्षेपेषु न स्वातन्त्र्यं, कामं दीने प्रोषिते आर्त्तिं गते वा ज्येष्ठोऽर्थाश्चियेत् । Harita.

"While the father lives, the sons have no freedom in accepting, giving or pledging wealth; if the father is in distress or is gone abroad or is suffering from illness the eldest son should look after affairs."

ऊर्द्ध्वं पितु पुत्राः रिक्थं विभजेयुः, निवृत्ते रजसि मातुर्जीवति चेच्छति । Gautama.

"Upon the death of the father the sons should divide the father's wealth or, during his life-time upon the mother being past child-bearing, at his desire."

These texts are a clear negation of the son's rights, not only to claim partition with the father, but also of any right of ownership in the sons. This view is perfectly consistent with the compulsory partition at the instance of the sons when the father is suffering from senile decay or a protracted and incurable illness, which we find indicated in some of these texts. But, as the text of Harita above shows, even here, the older opinion seems to have looked upon partition with disfavour. The more acceptable course was for the eldest son to manage the affairs on behalf of the father.

The next stage is marked by texts which deprecate alienations of immovable property by the father, *e.g.*, the following text :

स्थावरं द्विपदश्चैव यद्यपि स्वयमर्ज्जितं ।
असम्भूय सुतान् सर्व्वान् न दानं न च विक्रयः ॥
ये जाता येऽप्यजाता ये च गर्भे व्यवस्थिता ।
वृत्तिं तेऽभिकांक्षन्ति न दानं न च विक्रयः ॥

cited as Vyasa's text.

In the text as quoted in the *Dâyabhâga*, the last words are

"वृत्तिलोपः विगर्हितः ।"

"Immovables and slaves even if they have been acquired (by a person) himself cannot be sold without bringing together all the sons. Those who are born, those who are unborn and those who are in the womb, all look for maintenance ; there is no gift nor sale (permitted)" (or, following the version in the *Dâyabhâga*, "it is reprehensible to destroy their livelihood").

This text apparently marks the transition from the notion of absolute ownership of the father to that of co-ownership of sons. The immovable property (and slaves) is now looked upon as a fund for the maintenance of the family and it is considered reprehensible for a father to destroy the fund. Here the restriction is obviously in the nature of a moral and religious injunction only, it is not a denial of the father's right of absolute ownership.

This is however denied in respect of immovables generally in a text which I should place in the third class :

"मणिमुक्ताप्रवालानां सर्व्वस्यैव पिता प्रभुः ।
स्थावरस्य तु सर्व्वस्य न पिता न पितामहः ॥"

"Of the gems, pearls and corals, the father is the master of all. But in all the immovables neither the father nor the grand-father (is the master)."

So far, we find that the law-givers are seeking only to place restraints and limitations on the father's powers of disposition of immovable property, and that on account of the expectation of sons and grandsons to look to that property for their maintenance. As yet no idea of ownership in the sons and grandsons themselves has been developed. This however is developed in the last set of texts which marks the last stage of development of family rights and is made the foundation of the theory promulgated by Viswarupa and developed by Aparârka, Vijnâneswara and their successors. They are :—

"भूर्या पितामहोपात्ता निबन्धो द्रव्यमेव यत् ।
तत्रस्यात् सदृशं स्वाम्यं पिता पुत्रस्य चोभयोः ॥"

Yajnavalkya.

"In land descended from the grandfather, in *Nibandha* (a species of incorporeal rights) and *dravyas* (specified things) there shall be equal ownership of both the father and the son."

"पैतामहेत्वर्थे पितृपुत्रयोस्तुल्यस्वामित्वं ।" Vishnu.

"In grand-paternal wealth, the ownership of father and sons is equal."

This clearly seems to be the order of evolution of the concept which now holds sway over the greater part of India, thanks largely to the great authority of the *Mitakshara,* that sons, grandsons and great-grandsons acquire, by their mere birth, an equal ownership in ancestral immovable property in the hands of a person. It is not as if the evolution has been one unbroken continuous process. On the contrary, we find that at all the stages of evolution this doctrine has had to struggle against opposing views put forward on the basis of older texts. The struggle must have spread over a long time and it was carried on over a large continent. Naturally therefore the progress towards this end must have been a very complicated process. Even when this end was reached, the opposite view was quite strong, as exemplified by the views of such renowned jurists as Dhâreswara quoted by Jimutavâhana. And, even to this day there is at least one school of law, the Bengal school, in which the older theory, which I should characterise as distinctively Aryan and patriarchal, is strenuously upheld.

The progress towards the theory of right by birth and of the chracteristic joint family of Hindu law could hardly have been determined by purely logical or even economic factors. I am disposed to think that the example of non-Aryan races among whom the Aryans lived was a potent factor in developing the law of joint family.

The first important thing to note in this connection is that the strictest and the most logical joint family is to be found not in Aryan societies but in the Malabar *tarwad*. This is the true type of a joint family in which the right by birth of every member of the family in the *tarwad* properties is scrupulously recognised. If we can imagine that Dravidian society before its Aryanisation was organised on a similar basis, or at any rate that the Aryan society was at some stage of its history living in close and intimate intercourse with societies organised on the principles governing the Malabar society, it becomes possible to say that Aryan law was largely influenced by the example of these neighbours in developing a theory of family ownership.

The next important thing to note is that the concept of family ownership develops naturally in a Matriarchal society. It does not grow naturally in patriarchal families the cornerstone of which is the absolute authority of the father. In matriarchal societies on the other hand the male head of the family does not transmit his property to his offspring. He naturally falls into the position of a manager and trustee. The only productive members of the family are females who are permanent residents of the house. At the same time females are generally regarded not as owners or principals but as subordinate members of the family. They do not become owners and cannot divide the property. The only stable form of the organisation that can develop in a family with a permanent female population, who give birth to males who are entitled to enjoy the property only for their lives, is a joint impartible property managed by a male in the interest of the entire family.

Remembering then that Aryan society as depicted in the *Vedas* did not know of the joint family and that they were probably in close contact with matriarchal societies of the Nair type, it seems quite natural to suppose that Aryan society, when faced with the problem of reconciling the interests of the offspring with the ownership of the head of the family gradually approximated to the model of matriarchal families with joint ownership and adapted the institution to their own ancient notions. It is quite possible therefore that the peculiar type of family ownership which was developed in some schools of Hindu law was largely influenced by the model of societies of the Nair type.

INDEX